# Who is There to Share the Dream?

Finding Purpose and Potential After Tragedy

---

Dr. John M. Janzen

R & E PUBLISHERS ❖ SARATOGA, CALIFORNIA

**R&E Publishers**
P.O. Box 2008, Saratoga, CA 95070

*Typesetting by Diane Parker*
*Cover Design by Kaye Quinn*

Library of Congress Card Catalog Number: 91-050687

ISBN 0-88247-895-8

To Derek and Margaret

# Foreword

In a time where negative events preoccupy the attention of society, the individual's ability to focus on positive contribution is often lost. The author firmly believes in the capability of the individual to choose a life of positive contribution through utilization of personal abilities.

*Who Is There To Share The Dream* provides a view of different lifestyles reflecting personal choice or be acted on by external influences. Following each example, is a discussion on the meaning of choices made by the person with the recurrent theme reflecting the power of the individual to choose a life leading to personal gratification. The book is a strong statement of each person's unique power to create the happiness which they desire in this world.

# 1 The Essence of Living

Life is indeed an experience. What we choose to make out of each conscious moment is our choice. We can either experience exhilaration through adversity or gloom through success. The choice is ours.

No matter what our age, position in life, or experience, we are not compelled to retreat from life. Whether we are a child or grandparent, a performer of manual labor or an office worker, we have purpose. To determine that purpose and fulfill the meaning thereof is the reason for being alive. To do less is to deny the reason for living.

Each of us can be deceived by believing we have nothing to give. We can offer reasons for failure to support our opinion but not a single excuse. Our reasons can range from poor family upbringing to denied opportunities based on stature or intelligence, yet our belief has little foundation when acknowledging the host of personal abilities each individual has to create the intended life. Instead of paying individual attention to the worth of our deeds our ruler of success becomes measured against another person's standard of success. When we greet the person in the grocery store or on the street, is this act of kindness and generosity any less than contributing a large sum of money to world hunger? When flowers are accompanied by a visit to a resident in a nursing home is this act any more or less significant then hosting a telethon to raise money for the disabled? While each act is commendable, the bond between the object and the giver is the same element having touched the consciousness of the person to manifest the act of kindness. Each purpose has stimulated the person to act in a manner which draws the best that individual has to offer. To ignore the message which speaks to the soul or consciousness is to deny the essence of our lives.

As long as we breathe, we must remember our ability to give. We may never know the effect we have on another person's life by what we have said or the time taken to be with that person. Being in life is, however, not to be confused with existing, which suggests we allow ourselves to be treated as pawns by external events. Rather, we appreciate that the quality of life comes in many forms, and with a true commitment to our potential, unashamed and without fear we move ahead realizing through the actions performed in good faith will our life be enriched.

How simple the concept sounds and how much the initial desire to commit to using our potential. Yet, for many this commitment is short-lived. After a series of setbacks the former routine prevails and life once again takes on a stagnant existence of which we so desperately attempt to rid ourselves. We desired to make a career change, to free ourselves from the addictions of our dependent relationships, and to abandon our negative internal conversations which promoted failure rather than success. Unfortunately, the commitment to determine the consequences of our lives, either positive or negative was not recognized.

Too often failure, disease, and lack of productivity is blamed on external events, including economic conditions, childhood experiences, or lack of magic. In those instance where this attitude prevails, the life of the individual has been placed at the mercy of others.  At the very moment the person relinquishes control for making decisions to another entity, a part of that person's integrity becomes compromised.  While decisions are certainly influenced by the attitudes, actions, and responses of others, the choice to act rests exclusively with the individual.  Ironic is the tendency for many people to blame society or specific individuals for their failure while not realizing that they were directly responsible for giving up control in their life by allowing decisions to be made for them.

The belief in determining one's life begins in childhood and extends until death.  Of course, giving away one's power to choose ultimately ends with a form of death.  An illustration of a childhood experience may clarify the death of choice.  A man reported he was raised in a very structured household with a definitive picture of right and wrong.  The purpose on earth was to be good enough to get to heaven with a set of absolute rules to be followed.  The community in which he lived supported the same rules so there was a minimal likelihood of not understanding the accepted norm.  Further, there was little room for bending the rules given the absolute nature of right and wrong.  Everyone in the community knew those who were "out of the fold" and knew they were not "one of us".

Then one day this man left home and confirmed what he realized at an early age.  His view, while different from his parents and the community in which he was raised, was not wrong.  He found others who shared his views and encouraged him to seek answers to his own questions.  He began seeking answers to questions he was asking of himself.  He sought answers to reasons for his existence, to the pursuit of happiness, and to the effect of being raised in an environment where life was reduced to absolutes of good and bad.

For brief moments he encountered ecstatic feelings, followed by despair and confusion. He attempted to find resolvement of feelings in the lessons learned in childhood and became distraught for he had not learned to think, choose of his own free will, and accept the consequences of his choices. He realized that life to be lived would require starting anew as with a blank slate. Yet he had 18 years of experience which absorbed his mind and his heart was heavy. Later he realized the nature of this heaviness was guilt which to his credit was soon abandoned. He then resolved to use those positive experiences and discard judgmental actions and inferences which denied the value of human potential.

Shortly, thereafter this young man encountered a tragedy which would force him to live life on a day-to-day basis and occasionally on an hourly basis. Due to a leg injury sustained while playing baseball, he developed a bone tumor, initially diagnosed as malignant. For the next two years, surgery for removal of tumors, radiation therapy, and medication was a way of life. At a time when eight months had passed since receiving treatment for his last tumor and hope was beginning to emerge, X-rays revealed the presence of another tumor necessitating the amputation of the leg including the entire hip.

The consequence of a two-year period with an ongoing prognosis of six months to live resulted in peak and valley sensations of hope and despair. Attempts were made to find solace from within and comfort from others. When answers were not available from these two sources, contact with a spiritual force was attempted. He experienced, at that time, the presence of a force which transcended the personal dimension of life ordinarily available through his senses. This energy ultimately enabled him to manage the physical and emotional pain of his trauma on a daily basis. For out of that realization, there was a purging of the body, mind, and spirit which symbolized the shedding of skin. He realized his body was only the temporal structure which housed the mind and spirit which ultimately was responsible for determining his happiness.

During the time of acute trauma and pain when life hung in balance, his desire to live was unmatched in intensity from any other experience he had ever had. The fight for life became uniquely personal. Present and past experiences had a marked influence on him, particularly as to finding meaning for the pain and disruption in his life. Life events were no longer felt or understood as single isolated events but rather as something interconnected to a much larger whole. His senses sharpened and as the acuteness of his pain decreased the acute awareness of life's beauty increased. The smell of a morning, the smile on a person's face, and the color of the sky had a meaning previously unmatched. The value of these words are well understood as I write them, for the friend to which I am referring is me.

Obviously, there is a reason for each event which happens in a person's life, although some would suggest events occur for no apparent reason. While the causes or justifications for an event may not be initially understood, how the experience influences one's values and choices will determine the happiness with which that person lives life. No matter what the event, a benefit appears possible by considering the way in which life changes from our experiences and the lessons we learn. When a traumatic event occurs, whether this be loss of a spouse, job or friend, disease, or injury, there are generally two ways to respond. Either, we can give control to other people or institutions for our choices, or we can assume control for ourselves. While the latter choice may take more energy, ultimately the rewards are far greater for we know we have been true to ourselves.

Despite what type of experience occurs in one's life, each event has the potential to teach us how to live life. We can either adopt the vision of the eagle who sees the vast space of the universe, or the mouse whose field of vision is directly in front and minimally peripheral. For a balance of experience, both views seem necessary.

There are no simple answers to determining the meaning of life despite the fact that meaning is often realized through the most basic of means. A parent can have a most stressful day where every activity has been frustrating and where tension is at a bursting level, only to have the smile or the touch of his child provide an entirely different picture of life.

As we consider the meaning of experiences, we in turn learn about the truth of our lives which influences our decisions and actions. We learn that family, employment, and recreation are important. The motto in life becomes, "if it works it must be right". Our standard of truth becomes based on several general principles with few questions asked, unless major conflict develops between the person and the principles subscribed to. The person who grew up in a home where alcohol was forbidden and is invited to a home where wine is part of the meal must consider the truth of his actions and his beliefs of life. The questions must be asked, am I doing an injustice to myself, having a bad influence on others or doing what I believe?

The essence of life is far less the actual principles which we believe in, as opposed to the meaning we impart to those principles. For example, killing is justified by society provided there is a sanction from the government or in self-defense. Principles, in other words, become relative according to the norm of society, the beliefs which have been instilled by our family or culture, or those opinions to which we subscribe. Many blueprints for living are recommended from governmental, religious, and educational entities. Additionally, for as many individuals who exist there are likely to be that number of plans for living life. Each group or person is willing to suggest what should be done if you were them in a given situation. Rarely is it suggested "do what seems right to you".

In attempting to live a quality life, belief in the goodness of yourself and others is a prerequisite. Equally important is believing in the ability to create a satisfying life. The act of helping others is most difficult if not willing to help yourself. To deny what life has to offer and our ability to contribute to life is to deny why we exist. Tragically, many people have no concept of why they exist. They are consumers at best, taking from life what is offered with minimal thought of contributing to the quality of life, either their own or to others. Life is measured by monetary goods, which is not in itself destructive, until the person becomes the object of individual purchasing power or reduced entirely to the control of others. When one allows consciousness to become a free floating entity, shortly thereafter identity becomes hidden, because of one's control being snatched by those who feed off of others.

# 2 Determining Purpose

At some point within each person's life there has existed that spark of hope of what one would like to become. This hope could be called a dream, aspiration or longing. However one identifies this spark is not important. What is significant is the realization this sensation has existed or is existing and to act on information which is complimentary to realizing the fullest value of the sensation.

At an early age, I had some sense of what I enjoyed, what resulted in pleasure and what was uncomfortable. I knew that I enjoyed being with people and from a young age had some sense of ultimately being in a helping profession. While the manner in which I would use my potential was not apparent, I felt assured when the time was right I would know what to do. While the spark had appeared, fueling this spark was not readily possible as there were responsibilities on my father's farm. After all, there were weeds to pull, chickens to feed and field work to do. Additionally, the environmental conditions were not always conducive to pursuing what I knew was a calling. Life can seem very unfair at a time when driving a tractor in 100 degree heat (these were the days before air conditioned cabs) for eight to ten hours.

Yet each experience had a special lesson, for I was able to appreciate myself, and learn from others and my environment. During that time I began experiencing the acute nature of my senses. I smelled the fresh tilled earth and felt the morning dew. I observed the ecosystem in action, the bugs feeding off the plants, the birds eating the bugs, and on and on. I saw life, death and rebirth. The very important lesson which I learned was that every event in life has a purpose and that all life is interconnected. Through this realization, I understood every action I was capable of would have a positive or negative effect on other forms of life. I also recognized that ignoring my potential would be the greatest injustice I could do to myself.

In the years that followed was the realization of strength necessary for accomplishing a goal to include a strong commitment to be the ultimate best you can be, to develop your senses by becoming aware of each experience, and to recognize freedom as the most important trait to personal fulfillment. Also placed into perspective were the barriers which crept up along the way in the form of negative attitudes, financial constraints, and physical disability.

Most people will admit that they have dreams or previously had hope of becoming something which produces self-fulfillment. Through a process, often unconscious, the dream faded and life became a mundane phenomena, one which lacked energy. What happened? How did the person become removed from the dream? How did the purpose which seemed so important, become obsolete?

Perhaps the evolution of a dream occurs similar to the following form. First, there is a spark or a stimulus. Something internal or external touches our consciousness. Second, we respond by thinking about our sensation and trying to attach meaning to the experience. Third, we clarify our thoughts and feelings with family and friends. Fourth, depending on the response received from others, we develop plans for fulfilling the dream. Fifth, we began acting on the dream and, provided our experience is predominately positive, continue creating new goals.

The process sounds simple but as most know, only a small percentage of people realize one dream which has occurred in their life. Somewhere along the road, the price became too high, the risk too frightening, and the pain too personal. For those who believed that life was under their control, some were able to maintain this belief to accomplish the goal, and others lost sight and settled for something less or nothing at all. Yet others reevaluated their dream and started anew. For those who believed their fate was determined by others or external sources, a wave of discouragement and a sense of failure occurred when others were not there to give support.

The example of a friend who has not made the commitment to pursue the purpose which he knew himself to be capable of illustrates the life of discouragement when personal potential is ignored and fear is allowed as a mechanism to dominate one's life. This man, very conscientious, family oriented and willing to go the second mile for anyone, was employed as a manager of a small sawmill. The issue plaguing him was the fact he had graduated from college and instead of using his degree was performing a job much below his potential. Repeatedly, he lamented the fact his abilities were being wasted, yet he also was not willing to explore other options to utilize his education.

While nothing is wrong with performing heavy physical work, the attitude of this man toward being confined to a position which he considers a lower lot in life is tragic. His comments are characteristic of having been condemned to a position where his only alternative is to see how much better others are doing. The continuing source of unhappiness is settling for a position in life that he personally considers less than what he is capable of doing. While realizing the competency of what he does, his life continues unfulfilled as his daily activities remind him of performing a job which is inconsistent with a previous aspiration and contradictory to his feeling of purpose in life.

Why does this situation occur? Why is this man unable to put aside a job he feels is below his potential? Is it because of family or cultural programming? lowered self-concept? lack of employment opportunity? Or is the primary reason his expectations, daily messages he lives on, and the people he is choosing to make his dream a reality?

This man is not alone in his experience as many others share the same life story, only with a different content. The words "I can't" infiltrate their minds and hearts to the degree where these words become a reality. Life becomes mundane, for obvious reasons. The ability to think, feel, choose, and create becomes non-existent. Minds become closed to opportunities and tragically the dream disappears. Purpose is defined by past accomplishments with minimal thought to new experience.

To understand purpose in life, appreciation of the gifts we have to offer is necessary. Each person, whatever their position in life, has a gift to give which is unlike the gift of any other person. Of the hundreds of people which will be met in a lifetime, one's purpose should not go unnoticed, for if a gift is realized, an understanding of how we are to fulfill that purpose will become apparent.

A pleasure I will never forget occurred with a beautiful lady who, at 32 years old, was dying of cancer. Her attitude was no different since the occurrence of cancer than prior to the disease as she had always believed that her life was meant to be lived joyously. With a commitment to dignity for herself and her family she was defiant that the cancer would not conquer her. Not once since the diagnosis did she entertain the position that life was unfair. Rather, her entire waking moments were filled with living life to the best of her ability. Sadly she died several weeks after our meeting. Yet the attitude, commitment to dignity and self-esteem remained intact to her last breath. For this lady and for others, the end of a certain existence may be near, but the realization of purpose never diminishes. How truly remarkable the attitude in light of the personal experience of death occurring within her body.

Realistically, the question could be asked what does she have to give? At a time of severe pain and narcotics to withstand the pain, the appearance of a person twice her age, and dependency on others for mobility, the conclusion could very well be that she is no longer capable of giving.

Fortunately, because of her attitude that life was not reduced to mere physical existence and an attitude which holds if you are still breathing, your purpose in life has not yet been completed, she was able to live with dignity and reward for herself and others. Each person coming into her presence left with a different perspective on life. The discussion of death was not relevant, for life was what was important and consistent with her reason for being. She was able to laugh and cry with similar intensity as these emotions were consistent with what she considered true emotions of life.

Another young man had leukemia and at the age of 16 died. During a period of two years his cancer went into periods of remission, followed by acute flareups. During this time, he became discouraged, disheartened, and angry, but never gave up the will to experience life. While others had told him he was living on borrowed time, he refused to believe their proclamation and continued to maximize each moment he was awake.

In the last six months of his life, he lived an enriched life which modeled his belief that any attempt to ignore life causes the greatest injustice to you. The last time I saw him in the hospital, he explained how trees had become more green, the sky a deeper blue, and the air more energizing. He saw happiness and sadness in those coming to see him and realized the preciousness of his life in that experience. He remarked how with minimal physical energy, he was able to transcend his disease to give others an appreciation of life. The bond which attached him to his place in the world was the purpose he had identified for himself. As with the lady referred to earlier, he had resolved to recognize the sacredness of life and committed to making life meaningful for each person he met. Prior to his death, he was the visible form of an individual attaining the highest purpose of life by appreciating all that came to his senses. Since dying, his example continues as a source of inspiration for those who knew him.

The ability to recognize and use the gifts available is not easy, as the process is likely to be filled with many setbacks. For those overcoming disease, as with the two people just referred to, many life saving techniques appear dehumanizing. After all, body functions which are performed by equipment rather then natural processes, often accompanied by pain, can be a major obstacle which hinders the realization and completion of purpose, not to speak of maintaining a positive attitude.

During a time of trauma or setback, patience is vital. Each person in completing the quality journey will require a minimum of both patience and perseverance. There will be a time when the purpose is overwhelming and the energy has left. The parent at the end of the day who no longer has the strength to meet the demands of the child, the job seeker who has exhausted all possibilities and does not have a job, or the disease ridden body which fails to respond to treatment, all test the will to live.

Each person must closely assess those times of physical, emotional and spiritual letdown. Likely, the message which is being communicated is that we need a reprieve. In no way should our experiences be interpreted as failure, and in no way should we declare our dream is dead. On the contrary, the experience has value in that we are allowed a time to rekindle our hopes and consider the direction we are to move.

A time in my life when I had special difficulty understanding the significance of events occurred between having radiation therapy and learning that another tumor had appeared, necessitating amputation. For two years prior to that time, I had come from a lack of vocational direction to re-entry into college. My life had again taken on some stability as eight months had passed since the past tumor. I was convinced that radiation had destroyed the tumor as the length of time between requiring treatment had always been shorter, usually three to six months. Now the situation was far more serious as the tumor was back and very close to my spine and entering my stomach.

The loss associated with this type of experience is difficult to describe because words do not accurately reflect the sensation. The loss is felt in the body, mind, and spirit.

There is a vast vacancy touching the innermost parts of one's being. There is tightening in the body, numbness of the mind, and vacancy of the spirit. Purpose in life at that point is reduced to survival. The task of doing personal good is secondary to that of overcoming the acute pain of the trauma.

Fortunately for me, the shock was temporary and I was able to again manage my fear to where my hopes and dreams begin to reappear. Tragically, for some this does not happen quickly and even for a few, unfortunately never happens. In my life, purpose took the form of realizing that I may have six months or sixty years to live, but the most important point was that I was alive today. Once that realization had been recognized, I was able to see my purpose with greater clarity.

One other realization occurred which had a profound effect in recognizing the physical disease in me and my purpose for the future. At a time when my life was hanging in balance between life and death, I recognized the necessity of transcending my physical disease to consider the meaning of my being in the entire universe. The pain was periodically unbearable, yet there was a sense deep within me which seemed connected by an arc to objects outside of me. Not only was I able to handle my pain more efficiently, but this sense began taking on increased importance to where I realized a power in my life which would help accomplish any goal I desired. The emotion which accompanied this thought is difficult to describe other than a sense of knowing there is no adversity beyond one's control. Perhaps the analogy of the swimmer who does not fight the water but rather works in the context of his surroundings, begins to describe the experience.

I also experienced an added dimension of security. I became aware that terms of wealth, notoriety, and security were relative. In other words, they were defined by the person. The meaning given to those concepts was by the person, either based on past experiences, or societal standards. In contrast to having my purpose determined by external sources, including other people, fate, or the disease which had infiltrated my body, I chose to focus on the spiritual enlightenment which occurred from a set of stimuli or cues that I was receiving, all of which had the message "move forward". I knew I would not remain passive for I had realized the gift given to me, which if denied, threatened my very existence. How sad for the person who denies acting on a vision, dream, thought, or hope because of fear of future consequences. Many people will acknowledge the importance of purpose but deny themselves the opportunity of fulfilling the requirements or developing the appropriate attitude to meet that purpose.

I know a person who desires to be wealthy, yet the person flounders in each of his pursuits for wealth. A sketch of his actions will clarify why he has not become wealthy and, in fact, why he continually is in a financial struggle. Of primary importance to this man's failure is his lack of clarity toward the perceived purpose. First, most of his time is spent talking of his travels and experiences with others and the potential for those experiences to make him and others wealthy. While these projects are not necessarily well thought out, he does not lack for ideas and the discussion with him certainly piques one's curiosity. He is able to recite miraculous happenings which he has heard, seen, or been a part of, all of which are hard to dispute. After all, if a person survives a lightning strike who is to say they were not struck in the first place. Once the necessary support is generated the project begins.

Friends, colleagues and minor acquaintances turn out en masse for the ground breaking, remodeling, or whatever the project happens to be. Many are willing to help, although they are not necessarily sure in what capacity as they have not been told. The assumption at this point is that group energy will sustain the building process, so why worry about formalities of organization.

For several weeks the support is maintained after which time the commitment and number of participants in the project, which was designed to sustain itself, dwindles. As the final two or three people in the project make their gallant stand, consensus of opinion agrees the project was an idea before its time and now should temporarily be abandoned. Those last survivors, including the master proprietor, chalk up the experience as a valuable lesson for knowing what to avoid next time a similar project is considered.

In the preceding example, there is not an issue with the desired goal of wealth. However, for the man involved, there certainly is some question as to judgement and organizational ability. Equally important is the attitude toward himself as a person, his circumstances and his conclusions on how he will complete his goal of becoming wealthy. His purpose in life is to become self-sufficient, which to him means possessing those artifacts which money can buy. To achieve this purpose out of necessity he will require self-sufficiency in other ways as well. To achieve his desired goal, a sense that *he*, not the material possessions, represent control of his life, will be necessary. He will also require greater differentiation of those friends who can support his quest for self-sufficiency.

Not uncommon for people having a vision is to initially become very excited and share what they believe to be their destiny. The energy is exciting and others respond to this energy because the chord of excitement is striking similar chords in themselves.

The tendency at that point is to incorporate others into one's plans. Perhaps a support system or even a partnership is arranged. Realizing that consistency of purpose is shared by another person can be a strong incentive for accomplishing one's dream. For those involved, they realize a common purpose is being sought, and together the joint commitment will fulfill this dream to a higher degree. Partnerships can be beneficial, provided a sense of individuality is maintained by each person. The problem which often occurs is that others share the desired purpose only insofar as that purpose speaks to some need within themselves. When inconsistency of purpose arises, a time is necessary to appreciate each other's individuality and assess whether the plan for them requires modification.

Acting on what we believe to be our purpose should not, however, avoid the input from others. A constant reminder (which for convenience purposes, should be taped to the inside of one's forehead) is that all events, people, thoughts and feelings are set before us for a specific reason. To ensure that our actions are consistent with what we know to be our purpose is to seek those people who have risen beyond negative self-perceptions, learned to appreciate their gifts and acted on their visions. These people are easily recognized, for they are not talking about past accomplishments, but rather demonstrating their purpose by present behavior. The future is discussed only in terms of the next step in the sequence of completing their purpose.

How different our life could be if we used our senses to open our spirit and mind to create experiences. As opposed to an openness for what lies directly in front or to the side of us, we instead perfect our ability to dull our senses and roll with the flow by turning on the TV or radio for background noise which in turn prevents consideration to what gifts lie within us. No longer do we think, but merely exist, and then cannot understand not only what our purpose is, but how to fulfill that purpose.

The scenario just described unfortunately happens to each of us. Despite our convictions that life is well within our control, about the time our dreams become a reality, we nose dive into default. There may have been a comment from a friend, limitation of financial resources, or lack of job opportunity where the attitude of being victimized superseded any thought of how to gain from the situation by using our fullest potential.

Only to the extent that the person allows their visions to die does the dream become extinct. The commitment to purpose is lifelong. No one else on this earth has ultimate responsibility to their purpose but the person with the vision. The thoughts and feelings which accompany the vision are exceedingly personal. Accordingly, the fulfillment thereof will also be the ultimate responsibility of the person.

By allowing external forces to ultimately dictate our response to life we only ensure ourselves of a back seat in accomplishing our dream. The vision which lies at the heart of our purpose cannot afford to remove our strengths, capabilities and spirit in fulfilling the belief which we know to be true. As we begin on the quality journey each of us deserves, we first must realize we are body, mind and spirit where each aspect requires recognition, not to the exclusion of the other parts. We do no favors by filling our minds with enlightening philosophical information while denying our need for physical exercise or a nutritional diet. Recently, I became aware of a lady who began her journey of helping people by participating in many training seminars and reading as much literature on therapeutic approaches as she could obtain. While, in her opinion she was fulfilling the mission of her life, she began losing weight and for the last one and one-half years has encountered constant nausea. Obviously, one link in the chain of forward progression is out of balance.

Second, we must cultivate our listening ability. Good listening ability is one of the most difficult skills to acquire. Very easily can we become prone to selective listening. We listen more or less attentively to the degree in which we know a person, whether the person is family, friend, or acquaintance, and our interest in the subject being discussed. A simple awareness of watching a television program and having a commercial come on will clarify our own listening behavior.

Third, we must recognize each experience of our life has meaning to our ultimate purpose. Each sensation, thought, or feeling occurs for a very important reason. If our attention to experiences is of a selective nature where events are perceived as occurring at random, we certainly run the risk of excluding a particular event which can visibly illustrate our purpose.

Fourth, by recognizing that a barrier free existence is a reality a much more pleasurable life will ensue. Several years ago I produced a video entitled "I Can't Means I Won't" designed for helping individuals overcome trauma. The participants of this tape had experienced a variety of physical trauma including cancer and amputation. While the physical experiences of these people were noteworthy in and of themselves, the most unique part of the tape was the consistent message from each person that anything in life was possible. One man, in particular, who had all four limbs amputated as a result of an electrical accident and wore four prosthesis, recalled his interest in spending time in the mountains. When asked what he would do if encountering trouble, he responded, "call a mechanic". Each person, while having experienced both physical and emotional trauma, realized that they could transcend their crises to overcome any obstacle in their way. None of them entertained the concept of barriers. After all, life was to be lived by creating and focusing on the possible. Impossibility was a myth.

Fifth, to look beyond the initial stages of a dream is to create a strategy which maintains the dream. There is no virtue to desiring a position of prestige without some understanding of the consequences that accompany the position. While the president of a company may appear to have the ideal life with the perks of a corporate jet, exclusive vacations, and memberships in prestigious clubs, the time spent late at night assessing financial records or personnel problems cannot go unnoticed. There will be times when the problems of work or personal life are unbearable to the extent of wishing to give up the goal. The struggle of cash flow, marketability of service or product and devoting time to children can seem like a remote possibility. At these times, the importance of having developed a supportive group of friends or colleagues who can assist in continuing the path which compliments personal abilities to make these goals a reality is vital.

# 3 Believing the Dream

Many people with a dream fail to take any action because of a belief in the impossibility of a dream materializing. For them, the prospect of the dream actually happening is dependent on the correct combination of future occurrences or magic and the likelihood of their goals becoming a reality is remote at best. Comments of "when I get that promotion or win the lottery, I will buy that new car or build the house by the river", or "when I retire I will take that vacation" are conditions on which the dream depends.

Words of "if" and "when" have a tendency to keep dreams as wishful thoughts. Accordingly, these words must be eliminated if the dream is to be realized. The time for realizing a dream is now. Tomorrow only delays by one day what could be accomplished today. While future considerations and present circumstances are important, no less important is the realization that life continues to move, with or without you. That ultimate vacation, job satisfaction or family stability will never happen until a time in which you want it to happen.

Unfortunately, there are those who place greater value on why a dream cannot become a reality then attention to making the dream happen. Some use physical reasons as a means for being unable to pursue their dream. Others have reasons of family obligations. Yet others use the classic scapegoat of lacking personal ability as reasons why a dream is impossible. In listening to the excuses, one could conclude that life for these people is hanging by a single thread tied on the other end by the whims, desires and response of others.

I am aware of a couple who have worked very hard in their life; raised five children, and were a source of strength in their community. They have given of themselves first to their family and in no smaller way to the needs which they have seen in the community. If a person needed transportation to a doctor's appointment or required snow removal from their sidewalk, help was available.

For this couple these acts had some personal reward and were entirely consistent with their religious convictions of "love thy neighbor". Throughout their life the plan was to continue with these acts of generosity until they retired at which time, they would moderate their service to others and spend more time on themselves. While the acts of generosity came close to achieving total happiness, the happiness obtained fell just short of fulfilling their dream.

The plan was to achieve total happiness when they retired. For thirty years, the most important phase of life would occur at retirement, for at that time "we could do what we wanted". Up to the time of retirement, life consisted of survival and service to others. Now the day of retirement is at hand and to their dismay life continues as it has in the past. The fulfillment which was expected has not happened. There is still the if of tomorrow. To date, tomorrow has never come, at least not in a way which compliments their previous hopes.

The lifestyle of this couple provides a distinct look at why utopia has not occurred. Simply understood, they have not experienced a personal pleasure from making others feel good. Each deed has become a sack of commodities which is weighed against the expected reward. The more which is given the more is expected. The cycle becomes endless and true happiness never occurs. What they have not realized is the very act of giving can be a personal reward in and of itself, despite what the recipient of their actions may say or do. To believe that giving has a personal benefit, all that is necessary is to look at the unhappiness of a person who has lost the will to give.

One reason people give is because of the expectation others have toward giving. The poor, sick and homeless all conjure within us emotions which stir the heart and mind to give. While the need for each of us to share the human experience of self-sufficiency exists, there is a need to realize that giving must not be done in the context of guilt. Even the most callous person will feel the pang of remorse to see the face of a starving child. Yet happiness will not result if giving is done out of guilt.

Those who have learned to give unconditionally, without thought of what they will receive or more importantly with the realization that this type of giving provides the ultimate in personal satisfaction, have realized the act of giving is self-sustaining. Giving for them is done because they realize without a  sharing of their gifts, life would be lacking of a quality experience. In fact the basic framework of pursuing their dream is directly based on unconditional giving. Their beliefs do not derive from fear, guilt, or obligation, but rather an internal sense which in essence states "there is no other way".

The couple referred to above, who continue to live life in a way which provides sporadic rewards but not the exciting life they desire, reveals the aspect of fearing a different type of life. To have a life of excitement where one receives does not detract from the ability to give. After all, the more one receives, the greater potential there is to help others do the same. Yet, there appears a sense of insecurity where if they chose to receive, they would face a certain amount of guilt, either imposed by themselves or from their circle of friends. There is no doubt of their ability to change their attitude, which is necessary to pursuing a different lifestyle, however, foremost is to realize that they are worth the experience. Despite ridicule or judgement from others, without any acknowledgment of what they believe to be true, the happiness which they seek, will not occur.

Throughout my life I have found no value in exposure to people who preoccupy themselves with failure. The energy which is sapped from the mind and body is phenomenal. Continuous exposure to negativity places an undue overload on the spirit, notably when attempting to allow health and well-being to run its course. Recently, I encountered the vivid portrayal of a negative attitude when sharing the fact that I had ordered a car which I feel will give me great pleasure. In a conversation with several people, I discussed features of this car, particularly with regard to the happiness I expect to experience from driving this vehicle. Most people shared my happiness, however, there was one person who felt his obligation to point out that this type of car was notorious for mechanical problems with parts and mechanical repair being hard to come by. Further, if he were making the decision, he would obviously have bought a different car.

The importance of this man's response is not the disagreement over buying a car of bad taste, but the judgement he felt was necessary in saying that because he did not consider this purchase appropriate for him, how could it be appropriate for me. There was no acknowledgement that perhaps I may find value in having and driving this car, or the fact that I simply wanted the car.

Unfortunately, this type of response occurs far too often, whether based on jealousy, insecurity, or lack of understanding. For many people, this response dampens or even eliminates the start of a dream because of their lack of self-confidence in believing the rightness of their purpose in life. What was not realized by the man criticizing the purchase of the car is each person's purpose and how they choose to live their life, is uniquely their own. For some, having license over another person's life is easier than control of their own.

Beginning to live the dream requires an understanding that we have both uniqueness as a person and a shared experience with all of life. Consequently, any action we take must consider a unity with all other forms of life. The air we breath, the life we preserve, and the meaning given to life is directly determined by our actions. The choice is ours as to whether we wish to enhance or detract from life.

We must also realize the purpose we choose to fulfill must be in harmony with nature's way. To proceed blindly without regard for the rest of the world is likely to result in limited long term success. In contrast for those individuals having attained a personal state of accomplishment which they can define as success is a belief in the shared experience with all of life. Indifference holds little value. Whether a drive is taken in the country or a conversation is occurring over lunch, there is an alertness to the uniqueness and meaning of each experience as concerning one's purpose. There is realization that something can be gained and given in every situation which is encountered.

Philosophically, many will agree with the importance of believing humanity is but one force in nature which gives meaning to life and yet not understand the concept of unity which preserves life. They are able to observe the beauty of wild flowers with no comprehension of this beauty given the varied climactic conditions which are encountered and the implications to their own life.

Some years ago, while spending time in a primitive wilderness area of Idaho, I observed the survival instincts of many forms of plant life. As I reflected on these life forms, I realized they had endured many more hardships than had I. Despite a history of physical pain, and while my experience could not be equated with the columbine, I gained strength from looking and touching these delicate forms of life. I realized that the life as lived by these flowers benefitted from much of the same energy as me. Whereas I appreciated the warmth of the sun, so too did these flowers.

This experience also vividly enlightened me to how interdependent I was with nature. During this time I specifically felt an energy transferring among animals and plants to me and vice versus which was felt as a non-spoken feeling of warmth or low current electrical transmission. Perhaps the greatest realization in this experience was that every form of life had its place, and that a common bond directed toward the preservation of life held us together. At that point, an acute realization of nourishing life was understood.

The reasons why people choose not to share in life are as varied as there are individuals. For some, there is pride associated with individuality, others base their excuse on fear and yet others rely on their bigotry as a reason for not sharing. The person who states my project will be my own without the benefit of others, exemplifies the potential for the interplay of all three examples. What is not realized is that one's purpose and energy from others can be uniquely accomplished by also incorporating the involvement of others.

During the last ten years since my company was founded, I have repeatedly realized the importance of contribution from those employees who worked for me, the referral sources who educated me in determining how best I could be of service and the clients who helped me understand the realization that personal experience is never superseded by any other factor. During the beginning, my involvement in helping individuals overcome physical trauma was specially my responsibility. I was responsible for convincing employers, physicians, insurance companies, and others that injured or disabled individuals required assistance with planning and adjustment to the trauma they had experienced. I used graphic examples to illustrate the necessity of my services. The fact that physical injury can touch every dimension of a person's life in terms of physical pain, depression, sexual dysfunction, financial instability, and marital discord was illustrated as a uniquely personal experience.

I wanted an opportunity to live out the purpose I had perceived in my life and was convinced that, given the opportunity, I could restore integrity to those individuals I planned to help. As the number of people I worked with increased, the need to involve more staff became readily apparent. The addition of staff represented not only a change in structure from a one man business to a multi-staffed company, but represented some fear of being able to provide the quality of service which was necessary.

Through a period of trial and error, the staff selection changed to where there was greater consistency in approach and philosophy. Each person gained understanding that life for a person having experienced trauma is difficult and any attempt to assist that person must consider the totality of the person in terms of past experiences, needs and future interests. Central to the purpose of involvement was to educate the person on the importance of adopting control for their life, not only in the sense of survival but to evolve to a level utilizing their highest potential.

In retrospect, when considering the evolution of my company, I am amazed by the changes which have occurred from my initial thoughts of the dream. I realize that initial thoughts, sensations or ideas only provide a glimpse of the total picture. While the intended outcome may be initially understood at the time the dream begins unfolding, numerous mysteries are revealed which result in an assessment of purpose and conceivably a change of direction. When beginning my company, the basic service was to assist injured or disabled people return to a productive lifestyle. The dream of offering quality service, despite the complexities of each person, seemed simple enough. Yet the bigger the dream the more variations there were to completion of the dream, as I soon learned.

The first major complexity involved requests of referral sources which were not entirely supportive to the concept of rehabilitation which I subscribed to as being necessary to facilitate appropriate recovery. Due to injured individuals coming to my attention through insurance companies, attorneys and others, the requests involved consideration not only to the injured party but also those companies responsible for financial reimbursement, or issues involved in litigation.

Soon after beginning the dream the task became apparent that a wide variety of issues were involved. How naive, I thought, to think the process of rehabilitation could exclusively involve the injured person without major attention to the referral source.

To ensure consistency of direction in accordance with the dream, the decision was made to emphasize the integrity of the injured person and to restore control of life back to the person. That decision, above any other decision, has avoided many potentially conflicting situations when the issue of loyalty is at stake.

The second issue involved the increasing numbers of people who were being assisted. Within the field of rehabilitation, even performing the most basic of services requires substantial energy from the professional. Contrary to some perceptions, rehabilitation does not simply mean evaluating a person, assisting them to medical stability and plugging them into a job. Additionally, the host of personality factors influencing the rehabilitation outcome and the wide variety of options which require research and coordination to ensure compatibility of a plan places a timely demand on the rehabilitation specialist. When the numbers of injured people increased, there was a corresponding strain on the existing staff. The increase in numbers of people with whom we worked was planned and expected, yet unforeseen circumstances of employing the appropriate people, notably those who could balance their time in filling other's buckets and maintaining the level of their own and blending them into an organization, was no easy task.

The third and most complex issue dealt with the different and changing needs of those individuals served. Since beginning this work, the solutions to needs have required more creativity and analysis of options for meeting such needs. For example, to restore hope seems a relatively forthright goal until considering the concept of hope means something different to each person. Hope for one may be a job which represents financial security and for another maintaining a family relationship which depends on abstinence from alcohol or drugs. Yet if this factor is important to the services offered, a commitment to assist that person exists, necessitating at the least consideration to treatment and a plan which would meet that need.

Realizing that greater numbers of people served provides an opportunity for creative strategies, a video was produced "I Can't Means I Won't", which featured several individuals having overcome different types of physical trauma. The choice to produce this tape evolved after identifying the importance of hope for anyone experiencing trauma. There was also a realization that this tape would not meet every person's needs, however, the thought was to provide a ray of light which would counter the influences of negative thinking and a preoccupation with disability and disease.

Throughout the years many other needs have been identified and addressed through creative planning. Each time a need has appeared, there has been inclination or consciousness suggesting a solution. Several years ago, I had a friend tell me that we are never given a problem without also being given the answer. This statement would also seem appropriate to dreams, both during the initial stages and continuing throughout the life of the dream. Central to the reality of any dream is the excitement which occurs from seeing results and identifying new possibilities which broaden the dimensions of the dream. The vitality of life is surely enhanced when a sense of excitement and expectation exists to see what is around the corner or over the next ridge, and having the assurance of handling whatever situation appears.

Some people never begin to live out their dream because the "time is not right". The dream is conditional upon the children leaving, the job promotion, or retirement. There is never a wrong time to begin a dream. A dream and commitment to action begins with attitude and choice. Several years prior to my leg being amputated, I received a plaque from my sister with the inscription "Don't wait for your ship to come in, swim out after it". A better summary for commitment to action could not be said.

If I had waited on becoming aware of the importance of this experience until my prognosis was more favorable, three to five years would have passed before committing to a plan of action. What would I have accomplished during that time by waiting? Would my recovery have been enhanced? Twenty years later I am proud to say that not a minute of my life since that time has been wasted.

Not uncommon is to observe people merely existing. Life is mediocre at best, with few and far between thrills. The thought is if something good happens, it will occur in the form of being zapped by some supernatural force. When the force fails to manifest itself, the conclusion is that time is not appropriate, that the person is unworthy, or that one is essentially unlucky. With this premise that good comes from without, the high probability exists that one will be standing at death's door still waiting for the winning lottery ticket.

To experience ongoing reward in life, there must be acknowledgement of the necessity of personal involvement in one's happiness.  Security, happiness, and productivity are all within the capabilities of each person.  To believe one's dream is to commit to action and subscribe to an attitude of personal control.  While a degree of pain, despair and loneliness may be encountered, the commitment to personal control will soon offset the strain with such features as pride, happiness and satisfaction.

# 4 Living A Quality Life

I periodically meet people who state they are trying to define themselves and their purpose in life. Once this task is accomplished, to them the quality of life will begin. The idea of continually defining purpose is intriguing because of personal energy spent on understanding why choices are made as opposed to living life spontaneously and in good faith. As opposed to living out the values which are known to be true, there is definition and redefinition of purpose.

Recently, a man came to my office with a history of having injured his shoulder two years previously. Despite numerous medical evaluations and several recommendations for treatment, some of which he had tried, his life continued to be plagued by pain and waiting from one doctor's appointment to the next. For two years his life consisted of shuttling to appointments, all without the benefit of alleviating his pain or regaining control of his life.

When asked about his plans for the future, with a specific reference to a year from this time, he despairingly replied that he hoped "somewhere" there was a doctor who could help him. His life and control of his pain was completely relegated to others. The fact that previous treatment had not been successful was of little consequence to him. What was important was his belief that "out there somewhere" there was a magician who had the cure.

Many reasons account for why this person continued to experience a dissatisfying life. In part the reinforcement received for his pain was a contributing factor. Another factor involved the lack of consideration to his abilities as they could be used in pursuing a productive lifestyle. Yet a more important factor perpetuating his pain was his unwillingness to make the decision that his power could control his personal destiny. So basic of an action, but yet this very issue presented the greatest difficulty for him.

To look at the consequences of his life as being under personal control was one of the most difficult tasks faced by this man and others in a similar dilemma. As opposed to taking responsibility for controlling one's life is the decision to blame circumstances, lack of appropriate treatment, or personal inability for their experiences. To make a decision and face the consequences lies at the heart of our ability to live a quality life.

For good reason this man had an empty life because his entire identity had been turned over to the control of others. Accordingly, the first principle in living a quality life is believing in your capability to make decisions. Of importance, however, is that there is a time for thinking and a time for living out these thoughts.

To live a quality life is to appreciate each event represents some form of enlightenment, whether this be experience with family, work, or recreation. Living life with gusto, curiosity, and intrigue must develop into a way of life. Many experiences will be encountered which are ladened with stress, pain and uncertainty, yet the actual incident is secondary to our reaction or the meaning which we give to the experience. We can buckle underneath the despair of the event or we can react with hope for a positive outcome. I have seen both reactions many times. For those who live the quality life, there continues to be a silver lining reflecting many forms, all of which support the attitude that all things are possible. On the other hand, those who have developed the attitude that fate has dealt them the blow of death, life continues to be depressing.

Realizing life may have periodic failures, but with an underlying belief to overcome the failures, is the second principle necessary for living a quality life. One interesting observation over the last several years with people experiencing trauma is the difference which exists in their attitude for managing their difficulty. While frustration, despair, and anger are initially seen, for those believing in restoring the quality of their life the germinating seed of hope never dies. There is always the spark of expectation which glimmers in the heart and mind of the person. Experiences are sought which emphasize the positive, all of which rejuvenate the energy for their dream which was temporarily interrupted by a traumatic incident. The hope which they maintain is not blind, however, to their personal training. Realistically, they acknowledge the fact that life for them may take on a completely different reality as a consequence to their experiences. Life for the quadriplegic following a car accident cannot deny the physical limitations of the condition. This does not mean the dreams die. Rather by recognizing life will not be the same, but a new life can be equally, if not more exciting is the basis by which a quality life will be maintained.

The third principle to living a quality life which is vital to maintaining happiness and self-fulfillment is to seek others who share a similar belief system. Friends having their own quality life are able to radiate a feeling which is more powerful than any words spoken, although their words are likely to be very consistent with their attitude toward living a quality life. No doubt there will be times when the sky is gray, all friends have disappeared and the last ounce of energy has left the body. Yet these are not sufficient reasons to adopt the belief that life is ultimately against achieving one's purposes.

During the time when I was faced with an ongoing prognosis of six months to live, I was very fortunate to have a friendship with a man who understood in the value of being a friend. As a child we had grown up together as neighbors. School and work had taken us to different locations, yet we now were back in contact with each other for a reason which later I understood would have a profound impact on my life in terms of maintaining the necessary hope to overcome my trauma. At any time of the day or night, this man and his wife extended an open invitation to spend time with them. The quality of time spent in their home was most striking. While I was continuously bombarded by questions from others during this time to the nature and development of my physical condition, the time spent with these friends was not on sickness, but making the most out of life.

There was good seen in every situation. There was an electrical charge of energy permeating the immediate environment. Time spent on negative aspects of a situation had little value. Whether having a beer and discussing a political situation, or listening to a record, there was the underlying commitment to live life.

To this man and his wife I will forever be grateful. At a time when gloom surrounded my life, they saw beyond the darkness and revealed a way to transcend the clouds. A most intriguing aspect of the time spent with them is that the effort to talk of a quality life was not consciously deliberate. The words spoken and their entire way of being revealed the inner belief that despite a traumatic experience a choice can be made to choose the path which maintains the integrity of life.

How different my experience could have been if my choice for significant others involved a focus on the negative aspects of my condition. I am reminded of those situations when one person in a group has discussed the symptoms of their disease, only to have every member of the group feel sick by the end of the evening. Soon body parts that heretofore had not hurt suddenly begin to ache.

What is not surprising when the focus on sickness exists is the complete lack of attention to the other parts of the person which facilitate control of symptomology and one's life. Often no credence is given to the role of the mind, or heart and social or environmental events as having the ability to influence the trauma. By contrast, the issue of physical debilitation is so pervasive that any consideration to non physical traits is minimal at best. The power of suggestion is a strong potion for either maintaining sickness or health. Consequently, when a therapeutic environment is sought, choice of friends and acquaintances becomes critical.

A fourth principle to understanding the process by which to live a quality life is an appreciation of the network within the person consisting of body, mind and spirit. When an imbalance occurs with any of these parts, recovery from trauma and return to the excitement of life will be delayed.

The imbalance can be illustrated from the following choices. There may be a continuing focus on physical infirmity of what has been personally lost.  The friends sought out may be solicited to confirm how tragic the situation is.  The trauma may further be maintained for martyristic reasons.  The person may then choose to retreat and become isolated from the world.  As seen with these choices, the physical condition has received the attention to the exclusion of the mind and spirit.  Each choice has revolved around the negative aspects of the physical condition to a point where consideration of how personal strengths could be used in recovery has been buried.  Whatever the reason for continuing to place trauma in the forefront of life, anytime the focus is solely on the negative the road to quality experiences will always be filled with debris.

A fifth principle to living a quality life is developing a relationship with the soul.  The soul is an enigma, however, for purposes of definition the concept can be considered as consciousness or a source of energy which permeates all life.  The soul is both within the person and without, in other forms of life.

For those desiring quality experiences some realization of the energy coming from within is necessary.  This energy has a second component which touches all events outside of the person in the form of a reciprocal relationship.  In my own life, I have been continually struck by the encompassing nature of this energy as revealed by fresh revelations from many events on a daily basis.  Whether this energy derives from without or within is difficult to determine, the fact there is energy is what is important.

I find the smile of an infant, the assistance from a family member at a retirement center, and people of all generations feeding ducks at a pond, as events attesting to the prominence of an energy reflecting the soul. After all, there is something which touches the inner being of a person to appreciate these events.

Recently in a discussion with a friend, I suggested the relationship with the soul supercedes any other relationship because of serving as the basis for all subsequent relationships. In other words, the individual must learn to appreciate that personal part of their being, which is sensitive to joy, pain, and despair. Because of a relationship with the soul, there is opportunity for a quality encounter with friends, nature and virtually every encounter in life.

How different is the individual experience when the energy of the soul is denied. I recall a letter which vividly denies not only an appreciation of the soul but also any hope of experiencing a rejuvenation of what life is offering to this person. The letter begins with reference to a relative recently having his 70th birthday, followed by the opinion of the author that her life would soon be over and the necessity of getting burial plots at the cemetery. Then there was discussion of doing fieldwork on the farm but unfortunately the ground was too wet because of the recent heavy rains. The first positive point in the letter was on the second page where acknowledgement was made that the rains were good for the flowers. Hoping to feel the light was beginning to emerge, soon the discussion returned to what would happen to the flowers when taking a vacation in several weeks, as it was not possible to depend on others for their care.

Unfortunately, the writer of this letter likely has no concept of how her thoughts or the words she is writing prevent her from living a quality life. The central theme reflected throughout the letter is life provides only a marginal degree of happiness and yes, while good things can happen, there is a high likelihood that doom will follow. Life for her is permeated by the negative.How different this person's life would be if there was recognition that without rain the plants do not grow and by looking at the finality of death each moment of life can be given much greater value where each moment is lived to the maximum of one's ability.

I recall a time spent at a friend's house and in an hour or two vividly having the realization of life lived qualitatively. As we sat on his deck and discussed our lives there was a subconscious realization that both of us were living life as we intended. This realization was intensified by the excitement of his two children, ages four and two, who were filled with life and happiness. Throughout the late afternoon, other vivid portrayals of the quality life appeared. The two swallows, taking turns in the nest directly overhead, the playfulness of the dog, and the acknowledgement and greetings of neighbors as they bicycled or jogged by provided an exhilarating understanding to meaning of a quality experience.

None of these events necessitated momentary action. They did, however, require a much stronger investment of openness to experience which is a sixth principle necessary for living a quality life. One misunderstanding surrounding the belief in living a quality life is the necessity of magic. There is an element of truth in this belief, in that one never knows the ultimate value each experience can have on their life. The important understanding, however, is if experiences are perceived as magical, they are understood as being under personal control.

When life becomes disillusioning, the magical nature of experiences has probably left the person. Many people have stagnating or boring lives, simply because of fear associated with new experiences. There is loneliness but unwillingness to meet new people, job dissatisfaction but fear of changing jobs, and pain because of unwillingness to try personal control. A quality life by necessity involves risks. These risks need not be dangerous physically or psychologically but involve moving forward with an openness and realization that during the short time spent on this earth, life will be lived to the highest ideal. At some point, to work without a net may be a pleasure.

When working with injured employees who have performed essentially the same job their entire life, not uncommon is to hear the statements "I have put in my time; I'm tired; there is nothing to go back to; and I'm going to sit back and see what life has to offer." Their life at that point characterizes a hopelessness toward the future but also reflects a sense of having had wasted years from performing duties which were less than challenging. In contrast to using their abilities in their jobs, they essentially "put their time in." They reflect on the comments from irate supervisors, following schedules and dealing with unreasonable requests, all of which have produced a profound state of disillusionment.

On the other hand, the job has provided some rewards, otherwise they would not have remained for so long. Some acknowledgement is periodically made of the fear of changing jobs, but most often a greater number of comments refer to the negative versus positive experiences on the job. When positive statements are made they primarily involve financial incentives as opposed to internal or self-gratifying rewards.

The fact a person remains in a job for twenty years is not the issue. Granted, there are employees who maintain a life of excitement, at and away from work. There are others, however, who have perfected their callousness and believe that their entire life is programmed according to the standards of their employer. They are no longer able to feel, experience, or believe with any childlike fascination.

I have travelled around the country and spoken with many workers, those excited and those discouraged. The central difference, no matter the industry, is the belief these people have toward themselves and life. I have seen disillusioned doctors and lawyers, as I have factory workers. There are those, despite the occupation, who can smell the freshness of life in the morning, while providing technical expertise on how a generator works, and tragically there are those who have been dead to new experiences for years.

Why people avoid living the quality life they know is possible for them is difficult to answer. Each person in this world is comprised of different abilities, physical structures, and interests. Many reasons have been suggested for the cause of behavior. There are those believing we are predetermined, those believing we are directly responsible for our actions, and those believing one's life is a combination of predetermination and personal choice.

Each philosophical perspective likely has value insofar that the individual realize as a human being, there is always the option of choice. What is chosen in life can be attributed to many factors, including the availability of rewarding experiences. The central difference, however, for those living a quality life is their openness to new experiences and their decision to make and act on their choices.

# 5 Maintaining the Dream

Struggle is long but hope is longer.

There are days when the quality of life is reduced to a mere wish. No matter what is attempted, thoughts and actions just do not gel. Emotionally, a cloud of gloom persists. The thought is that previous accomplishments are secondary to what is being put into place at this time. The future is viewed with a sense of despair, although not to a point where hope becomes extinct.

To be stuck on dead center is not an entertaining thought for the person who has begun to pursue the dream. No matter what logic is used to describe feelings of letdown, including the classic explanation that these periods of gloom are natural and for purposes of reflection and introspection, the reasons are just not sufficient to explain the discouragement. While a block may indeed have occurred, the desire is for renewed inspiration. A reason for moving forward is the sought after goal.

Maintaining the motivation, interest, and inspiration for a dream to be fulfilled requires a full-time commitment. This is not to suggest that every conscious moment one is thinking about how to attain the dream. Instead, fulfillment of the dream becomes incorporated into one's way of life.

Approximately seven years ago, I had a dream which I felt would revolutionize the world. This dream involved construction of a sanctuary for rejuvenation which would provide a glimpse of the perfect beings we are. The purpose of the center was to educate, counsel, inspire and retrain. The center was designed for any person wishing to attain greater harmony in life through utilization of natural resources, including their own. After all, what I had accomplished on an individual basis was felt to be much more rewarding if pursued on a larger scale.

I soon realized this dream is somewhat analogous to creating world peace. While the goal is noble, the form in which the facets emerge to the person is likely to be dramatically different than initially comprehended. I found for my commitment to be maintained, the necessity to identify a standard of acceptance. In other words, what would I be comfortable with in stating that my dream was unfolding according to my intentions.

Initially, when electing to pursue this project, my efforts were directed to building a structure where body, mind, and spirit were blended with nature. Through harmony of site, principle, buildings and treatment procedures, I felt a haven for rejuvenation could be created. My delusion, however, was believing that the first task was obtaining a parcel of land with construction of a building. Soon did I realize a bare piece of ground does little to energize the human spirit. Without an understanding of relationships to nature and applicability to human dilemmas, the land would essentially take on minimal meaning to the purpose which I envisioned.

Because of an alertness to responses I have received on the nature of this dream, I have been able to see an unfolding much differently than initially conceived. Instead of preoccupation with a physical structure, there has been much more attention to acquiring personnel who are capable of rejuvenating others. This change of format has resulted in greater visibility of others being helped to recognize their ability to contribute, while releasing the potential in those providing the service. In this way, certainly in one absolute form, the dream is happening.

Despite a realization that the dream is occurring, there are periods of self-analysis when I wonder whether the dream is developing according to plan. I question if I am doing all that can be done. Am I reaching out to others in a way which is consistent with why I am alive? Am I fulfilling my purpose on this earth?

During periods of disillusionment, I conclude unfortunately I am not doing what I am fully capable of. This attitude likely relates to the mission I have identified for myself and reminds me of the fact that to whom much is given, much is expected.

I do, however, experience some encouragement by recognizing the fact that each experience in my life including my physical trauma happened for a reason, all of which served to increase my awareness for being alive and to be used as a source of strength in fulfilling my purpose. While I have not as yet built a physical structure, I am much more gratified to see the program which I conceived being put into practice, one which has at the forefront, human integrity. A perspective on personal well-being is much more gratifying than to see empty buildings on a sterile landscape.

Too often the energy for maintaining a dream fails because the recognition to live life between goals is forgotten. Despite continual pain, which has now been approaching 20 years, I have realized that life is filled with an abundance of rewards. This understanding is reason enough to pursue the dream. If a dream means to abandon all frivolities, a ticket for high blood pressure, or an early appointment at the cemetery, the time is necessary to re-examine the meaning to one's life.

Not long ago, a young man in his 30's came to my office as a result of a serious leg injury sustained in a car accident. The final result of his injuries left him with pain, numbness and weakness in one of his legs. After a series of treatments the final result was the need to rely on a cane for his mobility. His despair was quite pronounced over the fact that medically no additional treatment could be performed to increase his leg strength or reduce his pain. He questioned his ability to survive and doubted his capabilities for making a life comparable to the one he had prior to the accident.

While the injuries of this man are not to be underrated, the tragedy in his life is the attitude which followed his injury and has continued to this day. Sadly, he has equated the loss of physical mobility with the loss of mental ability as well. This man once dreamed of using his potential in a job which was self-fulfilling, and also a position in which his family could view him with respect. Some would say the accident caused him to lose hope and dissolve the dream. After all, how could a man who was entering the prime of his life adapt to a serious injury and hope to pick up the pieces?

This man has had four years with which to re-invent meaning to his life and has totally thrown his fate to the wind. He has no idea how he will financially support himself, what type of work he can perform, or what activities would improve his self-esteem. The meaning of his life and any hope of pursuing a dream is subject to medical technology, the availability of employment which would not result in pain, his attorney to arrange for financial solvency, and a host of other factors which would make his dream a guaranteed reality.

In response to his investment in making life fulfilling, let alone joyful, he responded "I have no control over that. Only time will tell whether I get better." Unfortunately, time will never help this man regain direction to the road of self-fulfillment. Tragically, he with many others will continue searching for that other person or situation to be responsible for his happiness and identity.

The example of this man depicts how tragedy can occur from a traumatic experience when one abandons hope. For him to achieve any appreciation of his power to control his destiny will require a complete transformation of his attitude toward making decisions. Without knowing how, he has mentally crippled himself to a place of being a pawn for others. At some point in his life, possibly by not choosing, which is a choice itself, he gave up dreaming and making decisions for himself.

As contrasting examples, there are other individuals undergoing acute physical and emotional experiences, who never entertain the thought of these experiences overcoming their purpose in life. Instead, the trauma is a teacher which serves in the context of a springboard, elevating the person's momentum and belief in potential to attain new heights. The trauma is viewed as a temporary event, only occurring for a short duration. As with other painful experiences, the realization is this too will pass. Not for once is the thought this trauma will beat me.

The example of courage, belief in potential, and a never say die attitude can be found in the personal example of a lady with cerebral palsy who, upon completion of a master's degree in rehabilitation counseling, and who, despite substantial physical limitations, never believed the dream of helping others realize their potential was impossible. A colleague and her former instructor, now reveals she has developed upper respiratory difficulty, requiring constant use of an oxygen tank to breathe. Has her interest in pursuing the dream to give and help others been diminished? Not at all. She is now developing ways in which to accommodate the breathing difficulty through use of a portable oxygen tank and a schedule which will maintain her strength to effectively help others gain meaning in their lives.

What a personal example of strength this lady is. At a time when the very essence of life, or the ability to breathe, is at stake, the trauma is still secondary to her ultimate purpose in life. The questions now concern how will I adapt to this inconvenience. Life in the past has meant living each day for the moment and now she realizes this fact with greater intensity.

As I tried to understand the experience of this lady and appreciate the value of her reaction, I considered my experience several years ago while walking around the lodge at Pikes Peak, Colorado (altitude 14,000 ft). With virtually any activity I encountered shortness of breath. My initial thoughts were varied. "Should I put a bag over my face? Would medication help? Whatever you do, don't panic". Fortunately, I remained calm, sat still and got off the mountain in a short amount of time.

As I came down to Colorado Springs, I reflected on the experience and wondered what form life would take if this breathing difficulty was constant. Would I make the most of the situation and realize, as did the lady referred to earlier, that this is just an inconvenience to adapt to? Or, would the decision be to seek a solitary existence relegating my needs to the care of others? For me, the decision would involve adaptation to maintain my independence. I have no desire to give up control over my life, until a time, if that ever happens, where control becomes impossible. At that time, however, I pray that the final decision will be mine.

A most unfortunate belief which develops when trauma occurs is that someone else is responsible for my problem. Looking for answers to ensure integrity from outside of one's self simply does not work. While others are helpful and necessary for providing a glimpse of who you are and instrumental in becoming the most you can be, the decision of how meaning is to be obtained for you, the person, lies directly with you.

Comments from those who suggest that dreams are futile can often be traced to choices they made to put their life in the control of another person or institution. Immediately, when that choice was made, a small part of them was lost. A part of the person's identify was compromised to the intentions of the other.

In my practice as a rehabilitation specialist, not uncommon is to be asked what type of work should I pursue? Should I have surgery? Should I retain legal counsel? These are certainly reasonable questions, particularly in view of the concern of the person, realizing their life has been seriously altered by injury.

The tendency is to respond quickly with suggestions of a solution, "Yes, you should get a job as an electronic assembler." "If I were you I would get an attorney." While these responses seem neutral enough, a very important precedent is being set by making these suggestions. At that time, the person asking the questions is at a vulnerable stage in their life. They need help and are looking for some alleviation of concern. Yet, without a careful response to their questions, slowly but surely, the decision of control is taken away from them and placed in the hands of other people. In other words, the person has become victim of the syndrome, "If I were you, I would do this."

There is a fine line between providing information which will help a person make a decision, and providing information which involves telling the person what to do. Most people whom I have met are quick to provide solutions to other's problems and have more answers for another than they do for themselves. Given the likelihood of this tendency to continue, the surest form of self-preservation is realizing that no matter what is suggested as an alternative, I the person, remain in control of my life.

# 6 Life Enrichment

Some have said that the human being uses only a minute part of the brain during a lifetime. This is not a consoling thought, when each day is filled with appointments, commitments, and a moderate degree of struggle. Little comfort is available by realizing that we may not be using our brain to the extent possible, when we are trying as hard as we can to give meaning to each day.

Even more tragic is to see the conscious moments directed toward limitations of the human spirit. For example, agreement with what is known, despite prejudice, as opposed to opening the mind to new experience. How often is heard after one encounters illness that the prognosis is poor at best. Pain is interpreted as cancer and the mind shuts down, periodically on a long term basis as a result.

What is necessary to have and live an enriched life? How can life be filled with a continuing sense of excitement, not with events which are the exception, but rather which occur on a daily basis including the work one performs, the conversation with family and friends, and the enlightenment from physical and mental exercise? In other words, how is a sense of the excitement attained or how can one be trained to understand that all of life can be exciting?

First, to appreciate the beauty of life, some recognition that life is beautiful seems necessary. This point seems simple enough, but how many of us would in contrast say life is a burden, life is hard, life is a struggle. Certainly, this would not be an uncommon response from someone living with arthritis or having recently become divorced. Yet many individuals experiencing these types of events observe a beauty by allowing new experiences to fill their lives and avoid preoccupation with excess baggage designed to weigh them down. The smiles of others, the freshness of the air, and the mind's intellect become far more important than belaboring the onset of cancer or the failed relationship with a spouse.

Second, as a prerequisite to living life with a renewed freshness to each experience is the realization that the human being has evolutionary capabilities. From birth to death, each person evolves to new levels of understanding which permeates one's life. What is realized in childhood is modified in adolescence and further refined or changed in adulthood. Each understanding gives a specific meaning to the person and is instrumental in shaping an identity. When the choice to stop evolving is made, beliefs about life and explanations of why certain events occur can readily be traced to the time when learning ceased to occur. How apparent to see the death of a mind in the person who chose to cease growing at the age of 18, in the decisions made toward family and personal ambitions. Having become closed to new opportunities, life is managed in a form consistent with the ideas of another age which may or may not provide the sense of happiness or excitement desired. The person who chooses to remain in a community which stifles creativity, when secretly desiring to pursue another profession and lifestyle, illustrates the means by which excitement is diminished.

Third, if life is to be enriching a commitment to experience is necessary. This commitment will not be easy, for the risks of failure often outweigh potential successes. How sad to see the person with a low back injury talk only in terms of limitations with no appreciation of mental or emotional capabilities. For life to have new meaning, the old thoughts of having learned everything must be abandoned and replaced with a sense of curiosity. Additionally, the fear that on the other side of the hill there exists something worse than presently exists on this side must be discarded until the trip over the hill has been made.

Fourth, the need exists to realize the sacredness of life and understand that each event which transpires is there in the capacity of teacher. I never ceased to be amazed by the comments made by friends who are excited by life. Their observations may reflect any of the senses but always depict an energetic quality. For some the cloud formations, the quantity of pine cones on certain types of trees, or the color of the sage in the spring is the energizing quality of life which provides the sense of excitement. For others, architectural design which accommodates the landscape or the quality of personal interactions maintains the richness of life. The common bond among these people is that whatever event is presented to them, the most will be made out of their experience.

Fifth, a sense of imagination is important to living a zestful life. To realize the truth of this point, one need only to see what the presence of a child does to a group of people having a serious discussion. The life and vitality in the small body quickly creates a feeling of energy which infiltrates the entire group.

Not long ago I was waiting in the gate area of my plane to leave when a young couple with their two year old daughter appeared on the scene. Prior to the arrival of this young child and her parents, most of the group of approximately 25-30 people were involved in traditional airport behavior consisting of people watching, novel or newspaper reading, and perfecting the blandness of their appearances.

As is known by anyone having had a two year old child, the task of keeping the child sedated, let alone in an airport, is a most difficult task. Fortunately, her parents were relaxed and felt no fear in allowing their daughter to entertain the rest of us serious people. Within 10 minutes, as I looked around the gate area, three-fourths of the group had smiles on their faces. They were now making a connection with the vitality of this child who ran from one person to the next, telling them that she was going from Salt Lake City to Seattle.

As I considered the impact this child had on me, I realized how refreshing the feeling of living for the moment is. How beautiful the life to not be directed by hate, fear or mistrust. What a pleasure to see a spontaneous reaction without the interference of ideology. As I later sat in the plane I realized that a choice so simple to make for the pleasure of all is often the last choice to be made.

In my rehabilitation practice I never cease to be amazed by the profound efforts and tolling energy spent by clients on avoiding spontaneity. Interestingly, there are a number of professionals where this is the case as well. The pros and cons of taking a step forward are continuously weighed, evaluated and re-evaluated to a point where the issue at hand has become distorted and the poor individual increasingly depressed. The options available have become so muddled in the mind that no action at all seems more comforting than any previous options considered.

The experience of a man whom I have worked with for a year illustrates the negative consequences, when the ability to act is denied and when spontaneous action is a remote possibility. This man was referred for rehabilitation services due to a back injury and the inability to return to his employment as a construction laborer. During the initial evaluation, he complained vehemently of low back pain and expressed his frustration over the medical treatment received to date. In his opinion, the physicians whom he had seen were insensitive to his complaints and less understanding with their procedures and recommendations.

Combined with intense ongoing physical pain, this man had now fallen victim to a far greater defeat in terms of a life without goals. The beginning of each day was filled with thoughts of "how will I get through the day." "What will I do until my kids get home from school and my wife from work?" "Then, what will I talk to my family about." Generally, this man's life was rooted in the depths of despair.

As is my initial approach with every individual having sustained trauma, I attempted to provide him with a sense of hope. Time was spent reviewing his medical history and the implications of treatment to his life. His educational and employment history was thoroughly reviewed with him in an attempt to provide an understanding that he had acquired skills which could be used in a variety of ways, either in directly returning to work or pursuing additional training. His social and family relationships were discussed to highlight his strengths and develop a support system.

Unfortunately, suggestions for use of his ability were met with negative responses from him. Each response reflected a doomsday mentality with connotations that the only way success could be accomplished would be through a major miracle, through which he of course would have no control. His responses were predicated on what he had been told by others, his perception of his physical condition and the options available to him, and his desire to maintain the hate he felt for those having treated him.

The reaction of this man sadly is not atypical to that of others who believe they are in the same boat, drifting out to sea. Through my experience I have found that this reaction can only be maintained as long as the person commits to this belief and has reinforcement of the behavior. The contrasting example of those others who commit to a life of vitality confirms that another more productive option is possible.

When laboring with a person to show the way of hope, a tremendous amount of patience is necessary. Often found with a person who is unconvinced of any potential is a cumulative effect of negative life experiences, all of which support the concept of inability. Every suggestion of hope is countered with a response of why this action will not work based on one or a host of previous experiences.

During my 15 years of professional rehabilitation practice, I have encountered virtually every conceivable excuse for avoiding responsibility and using one's potential. However, about the time I believe that the most imaginable response has been given, one other comment will be made that supercedes the rest. Excuses to the effect that "I will die", to being an "invalid and living a life of destitution" are not uncommon as reasons to avoid taking responsibility.

The responses seem to have one theme in common, reflecting the fear that taking responsibility will result in a worse life than what presently exists. There seemingly is a part of human nature which believes that trauma is inevitable and recovery from trauma is filled with pain and more trauma. When asked why they have not moved on with their life, often the response is that moving ahead would only result in unforetold dangers. Whether the trauma involves remaining in a bad relationship or allowing pain to be the god of life, not taking the step to look beyond the horizon has devastating consequences for the individual.

One person, several years ago, stated the only reason she had not returned to work was that her doctor has advised her to get plenty of bed rest. Two years later she was still adhering to the orders, by remaining in bed 16-20 hours a day. When asked if she was happy, she flatly stated, "happiness is not the issue. What I'm doing is following doctor's orders to save my life."

As much as the tendency exists to hold on to negative perceptions and maintain a life of inactivity, one would think the individual is receiving some mileage out of these choices. While there is little doubt that we have developed a system for compensating the person according to the degree of sickness, the price paid by the person is unmatched. Essentially, no value can be placed on the emotional turmoil existing within the person on a daily basis. The closing in of walls, the observation of other people being active, and the realization that personal potential is wasted serves as a constant reminder of one's lack of productivity. Despite the fact that those of us coming into contact with individuals holding on to disbelief is no picnic, the experience of the person with the trauma is far worse, unless we as a spouse, friend, or relative assume responsibility for this person.

What a contrasting experience of the person who says, "Yes, I have been told of my cancer, but I will continue with the vigor of life as I have before." Some years ago I recall watching a television program featuring a lady who quite early in life had been very successful both professionally and personally. Professionally, she had been an actress and previously won an Oscar. Personally, she had married and raised five children. Following the raising of her family she experienced three strokes. Her prognosis was poor for recovery. Yet here she was on stage, stating that she has a richer life now than she did prior to encountering physical problems. As she related the meaningful events of her life which had the strongest contribution to her recovery, she believed her spirit and the support of her family was most significant.

The experience of vitality exhibited by this lady and others having chosen a life of excitement is the commitment to never say never. Barriers are only in effect until a way in which to overcome the obstacle is identified. A most interesting feature to the personality of these vital individuals is that rarely is there bemoaning of predicaments. Instead, very effectively they subordinate their problems to the use of their abilities.

For the individuals choosing to live a quality life, there is a tuning out of the negative. Initially, the process to disregard those "I can't" statements made by associates or acquaintances may not be easy. However, once the destructive value of those statements is understood the process for avoiding these contacts is as similar as to giving up carbonated drinks when having an ulcer.

Perhaps there are those people who must have a problem to feel important. I have unfortunately met people who insist on discussing their illness over their attributes. These people are easily recognized for they are the most verbal in a group discussion on illnesses. They are aware, although very superficially, of the latest research to solve the problem which obviously is a pill, injection, or treatment outside of the person. The power of personal control seemingly has not grasped their attention.

Those wishing to maximize life through personal efforts, on the other hand, can be seen by taking initiative on their own. They do not deny the limitations of their illness or disability, but instead of reaching for the magic wand outside of themselves, seek to obtain the solution from within. The solution involves mobilizing the internal power of belief and striking the arc of energy from within to those outside who reciprocate in illuminating their potential.

During the first several years after having my leg amputated, many acquaintances would inquire as to the nature of my progress or whether I had any recurrence of cancer. I was struck at that time by the lack of comments made about aspects of my life, other than cancer or the amputation. People wanted to talk trauma. The bizarre experience of cancer and amputation was worth higher coverage than the fact that I was continuing my education and pursuing employment. When bringing the issue of my productivity to their attention, not uncommon was to be dismissed with a simple statement of "that's nice", followed by a return to discussing an unfavorable prognosis.

Based on my present observation of people experiencing physical, psychological, or social trauma, today the predominant reaction appears no different. The plain fact is that a much easier time exists discussing what is wrong versus what is right in a person's life. Not once to my recollection, when I resumed my junior year of college after the amputation, was a comment made of the strength demonstrated by the commitment to be productive.

Tragically, for many a life of unhappiness is the norm, where happiness if realized at all, occurs only for brief intervals. They cannot understand why they remain victimized. "Why," they ask "do I continue with my pain?" Perhaps the answer is so close at hand that they are unable to see it. Simply, by maintaining a focus on pain, disease, disability or unacceptability, they cannot hope to return to a life of quality. By holding on to this focus, life cannot help from being dictated by these principles. How can one recuperate, when the cancer of negative thoughts infiltrates the body, mind, and spirit?

## Phase I—*Identify Your Skills*

For those desiring a quality life, the road to enrichment is unfamiliar. The questions are asked " How do I begin creating quality experiences?" "How do I live a quality life?" "Where is the map to show me the way?"

Despite sincere attempts to overcome the negative influence of trauma, failure, and pain, the life of quality continues beyond the reach of the person. After repeated attempts to improve one's position and after resolving to avoid the emotional turmoil without success, the price often becomes too high to pay and the alternative of giving up is chosen.

There is no question that living an enriched life takes energy. Although some are seen living a life of vitality with little personal effort, most of us are not handed a free ticket to ride on the luxury liner of life. For the vast majority there are jobs to go to, children to attend, and bills to pay. Yet there are those with these responsibilities who live joyful lives and with a renewed freshness each day. These individuals have grasped the meaning of participating in life fully and utilizing their skills to the best of their abilities.

When encountering people who are bored with life, not uncommon are statements that they have "thought and thought" and still cannot determine a viable alternative for increasing the quality of their life. Despite substantial time devoted to thinking about life, the gelling of thoughts has not resulted in a more satisfying life. The basic activities of life for them essentially continues as they have in the past without much change of venue.

The problem for these people is that they continue to function with a life script which is designed for a life of mediocrity. The skills and behaviors relied upon presently are designed for only a limited amount of enrichment. By continuing to restrict the group of friends, reading materials, and radio programs exposed to on a daily basis, minimal opportunity for growth and new experience is possible. However, by diversifying experiences on the other hand, opportunities for enrichment readily become possible. How much more enriching by planning a vacation as an adventure as opposed to a basic sightseeing excursion.

A starting point for those individuals desiring to experience the spirit of life is to identify their personal skills and abilities. Questions of "what am I good at?" "What have I learned?" and "What am I doing for my livelihood?" are questions which will begin a life of enriched quality.

Many people experiencing trauma develop the feeling that along with the trauma, they have lost every ounce of skill or ability ever possessed. While the effect of depression cannot be discounted, to think of losing mental capability after having a back injury is ludicrous. Yet not uncommon is to hear that my back was my life and in some unforeseen way directly connected to my judgement, memory and decision making ability.

This reaction unfortunately is not limited exclusively to those experiencing physical trauma. Equally intense reactions occur from those having been divorced or terminated from their job. Instead of a body part being the vine of life, the previous spouse or occupation now becomes the all important factor which has brought life to a standstill. The significant other now becomes the body, mind, and spirit for the person.

To reverse the tendency to equate the meaning of life with a lost body part, body function, ex-spouse or job, the conscious decision must be made to recognize yourself as a person with abilities and capabilities. As human beings we are born with the ability to think and feel. As we grow we develop our skills and reactions to a host of complex situations. These experiences result in learning of skills to adapt to specific situations. Of particular importance is to not ignore these skills during traumatic times.

With many individuals I meet, the history which reflects their life is one of strenuous physical work. They literally have worked with their hands and back and have relied heavily on their physical capabilities. When recognizing they cannot return to their customary work, there is ordinarily a period of despair or depression resulting from the feelings of loss associated with being unable to return to an activity to which they are accustomed.   They also have the majority of attention placed on their pain and physical limitations with little or no attention to their attributes, which does not help overcome a negative emotional reaction.

The scenario for the vast majority of these people is that given the physical nature of each job they have had and the limited amount of education to obtain something lighter, they now are incapable of securing employment.  Up to this point, their attention has been centered on their physical condition, with perhaps remote consideration to their skills and future employability.  Even less consideration is given to the productive potential within them.

In a professional sense, the task is to clearly consider the implications of the physical disability, but also consider such aspects as psychological makeup, both emotional and mental, social and family history, hobbies, vocational activities, education and any special training, military experience and any other factor which would lead to an identification of skills which will return this person to a quality life.

The consideration of these factors by the individual experiencing the trauma is often foreign.  Reactions vary from total disbelief in capability to anger at having suggested that possibly there may be more to the person besides flesh and bones.  Most gratifying, however, is to observe the reaction of the person to realizing that "Yes, I do have skills which can be directed to a wide variety of activities."

As I observe the manner in which a person considers the aspect of personal skills, I am amazed by the limitations which are imposed on life.  For example, if a man is 45 years old, has a 9th grade education, a history of employment as a mechanic, and lives in a town of 15,000 people, why because of a herniated disc (back injury) is he considered totally disabled?  What became of attention to such aspects as this man's motivation, his desire to provide for his family, his conscientiousness toward employment and his ability to relate to others?  Are these latter factors any less significant in helping him return to a quality life of productive activity then the fact he cannot lift 50 lbs. or crawl underneath a car.

The sad truth is that the majority of attention in his recuperation will focus on treatment of physical factors. There will be multiple forms of evaluation, diagnostic tests, and inordinate attention to the physical ramifications of the injury.  The programming of physical function will be intense, the comments by professionals and reactions from family and friends ingrained, and the emergence for the person of a life of inactivity.  Only by considering the other parts of life and most importantly the fact that a life of quality is possible will the negative outcome be combatted and hopefully avoided.

Of necessity in addressing reaction to trauma is to acknowledge the intensely personal experience of any trauma.  No doubt there is difficulty focusing on spirit and highlighting one's skills, when physical or emotional pain supercedes any attention to these attributes.  Yet, each of our conditions will stabilize at some point to where we can devote a serious and consistent focus to utilizing our abilities.

The emergence of skills is manifested in as many forms as there are people in this world.  There are those individuals with ability for mechanical activities, deductive reasoning, working with the public, communicating ideas, and calculating numbers.  The list could continue endlessly.  The importance is not to compile an all inclusive list of potential human activities as is the task for each person to identify the skills which he or she possesses, followed by determining how best these skills can be applied. The road map lies within us, only for us to plot the course.

## Life Enrichment Proportional to the Degree of Joy Desired from Personal Activities

Those individuals maximizing their lives appear to have the motto that "anything worth doing should be fun." The distinct difference between the person enjoying life and the person for whom life is a monotonous struggle is the choice made to have fun and the decision to convert experience into pleasure.

Choosing joy for personal experience is a way of life. Not only are daily experiences perceived as pleasurable but choices made for friends, relationships, employment, and extra-curricular activities are based on the premise that life is to be lived in the context of joy. The meaning which is created by the person has a right which needs no explanation. The feeling of joy is there because that which creates joy is understood as the ultimate purpose for being in the world.

How different is the person who, by choice, restricts the availability of experience and limits the pleasure from each experience. I am amazed how often I hear comments of "Thank goodness it's Friday," and on Monday morning the same people bemoan the fact that they must go back to work. If I lived that kind of life, I believe I would soon realize what a waste of time to work. Somehow, I would pay closer attention to what I was doing and feeling from Friday evening until Monday morning. Perhaps, attention to that period of time would give me a clue to having a happier life.

Many years ago I made the decision to avoid situations which were unproductive and remove myself from feelings of indifference. I considered my productivity and the opportunity to experience joy in life in the highest regard. My hypothesis was that if I would approach life with a sense of openness and joy I could also elicit that reaction from others.

The practical aspect of that belief has produced a variety of reactions. For those understanding the value of joy, they have responded with vitality. The meeting between us has been a celebration and rejuvenation of life. There has been the electrical charge one receives from the sensation of skiing down a mountain on soft snow on a clear winter day.

Then there are those who have long abandoned the realization that maintaining a belief of joy for personal experiences creates a more gratifying life. Skepticism versus spontaneity has been the reaction. While they would like to believe that the experience of joy is possible, they consider this possibility only in terms of a carnival mentality. "How," they ask "can life be one big party?" Even more important, "how could I allow myself to truly have fun?"

Not long ago I was having dinner with a colleague in a very fine restaurant. The atmosphere, food and service was exquisite. The restaurant had no barriers to personal interaction, as the tables were designed for parties of 4-8 and the booths for conversations between two people.

Adjacent to where we were sitting was a group of seven people, three men and four ladies. During the course of the evening the conversation and humor at the table became animated to a point where those of us at surrounding tables could not help but notice the reactions of the people at that table. (In fairness to the restaurant the noise was not at a decibel level to interfere with the dining pleasure of others). After several glances over to the table I noticed that four of the seven were involved in the conversation and the other three had the appearance of dazed spectators. They sat at one end of the table with sober looks, while the other end of the table carried on. Only after the meal arrived was any movement observed from the other three, although not in participation of laughter.

As I left the restaurant I thought about the difference in experience for these people. Perhaps the three who did not share the humor of the evening were not incapable of experiencing joy, but simply failed to see the humor of that situation. I have been at dinners where I felt like a spectator behind a glass while a conversation carried on the other side of the table. The experience is not pleasurable. Yet for an hour no demonstrable signs of vitality emerged from those three. In fact as opposed to pleasure was the observation of sadness in their faces, which seemed to depict that the experience of that evening had not been the first of its kind.

Living life with joy and pleasure should not be misconstrued into the perception of a continuous beach party. Joy is experienced in a variety of overt and subtle forms which is characteristic of our diverse natures. Some of the most meaningful experience I have had occur from gaining understanding of a situation which enlightens me toward my ultimate purpose for existing. Whatever the choice for meaning and joy over the death of productivity is a decision which requires recognizing we have the control circuits and switches within us to experience pleasure and the sooner we wire ourselves to the creation of pleasure, the more profound our lives will become.

One danger to dashing the experience of joy is falling victim to the belief that we are not worth this experience. Many still maintain the destructive belief that if it feels good, it must be a sin. The belief goes on to create little scripts of "I can have a little fun, but not too much," or "I will be punished for feeling good." Soon these tapes transfer into creation of personal limitations where pleasure is destructive to the ultimate purpose of life. In essence a little hedonism is fine but only if it is done twice a year.

The experience of joy has many rewards, but perhaps the greatest is the manner in which joyful experiences bring people together. Happiness, vitality, empathy, gratitude, are all characteristic of a joyful experience. The choice to experience without fear cannot be matched. What a pleasure to believe in our ability to handle every situation either through personal attitudes or mobilizing the abilities of others, and deny ourselves to be victimized by archaic falsehoods building on human limitations.

## Finicity of the Human Body and Infinicity of Human Experience

Realizing the reason and meaning of experiences has been a most misunderstood phenomena in life, particularly when the experience is traumatic. "How could this happen?" "What did I do to cause this to happen?" "Why am I being punished" are often asked questions. The need to explain, rationalize and justify seems to be an ongoing human predicament.

As I observe tragedy and treat those individuals having experienced trauma, I am inclined to believe certain definable limits exist with the human body, but not limits, other than placed by the person, exist with the spirit. There is no question that as an amputee, certain activities of life are not reasonable. I will have a hard time running the mile in 8 minutes, navigating a horse in a full gallop (and actually staying in the saddle) would be a test, or walking a tight wire. I have realized, quite simply, that my body by virtue of the amputation, has definite limitations. These limitations, however, are fortunately superseded by my imagination. My imagination can be vividly observed in watching me on the dance floor. While my leg and upper torso work with the motion of a robot, I soon loose preoccupation with physical movements when my spirit of vitality takes over. I recall the second or third time I attempted to dance after my amputation (the first was a disaster and filled with how I looked on the dance floor) and the ease I felt in the experience. While having a vague awareness of my body playing out a series of motions, the realization of the music flowing through all sensory receptors followed by the joyous sharing of the experience with others on the dance floor, preempted my physical being at that moment. Certainly, there were times when I hardly moved, nonetheless the experience of the moment was one of life. The physical nature of my being, while obviously having physical limitations, particularly in a jitterbug sense, had no effect on my happiness by virtue of my choice to experience that night.

I have seen other individuals with observable physical impairments make the choice to live and live to their maximum capacity in similar situations. Just because the paraplegic is confined to a wheelchair is no reason why they should be removed from participating in dances or sporting events. Provided they do not roll over my foot with a wheel, I have no fear of being on a dance floor with them. Frankly, I have seen the music fill the soul of a person in a wheelchair to the same intensity as those who are ambulatory and fully capable of using their legs.

In the practice of rehabilitation, one of the initial and most persuading influences of injury is the ongoing physical limitations imposed by the condition. The amputation, malignancy, spinal cord injury, and muscle disease are all graphic reminders of the temporal nature of our bodies. The body, by virtue of age, trauma, and lack of immunity, is subject to these impositions, provoking the realization that despite our wish, we are faced with the likelihood of inherent physical limitations.

While each person I have met has some physical or mental limitations in comparison to others, the degree in which these limitations manifest themselves to the person or in the world depends primarily on the individual. Certainly, there is medical intervention which can offset the limitations, yet when assessing the severity and duration in which destructive symptomology is allowed to exist, the choice, when analyzed, clearly lies with the person.

A man whom I evaluated for purposes of developing a rehabilitation program illustrates this point. This individual experienced a back injury approximately two years prior to our meeting. Since the injury he has seen four physicians, all of which have recommended conservative treatment, to include physical therapy, medication, and exercise. None of this treatment, in his opinion, has significantly reduced his pain. Surgery has been considered, although he is not willing to entertain this option until being on the brink of immobilization. At this time he has no idea what ultimately will reduce his pain or what goals he can look forward to a year or five years from now. His only realization outside the physical realm of his experience is that his employer ultimately will pay for the injury which irreparably damaged his life and some understanding of the effect of his altered life, in terms of tension and frustration for himself and his family.

The preoccupation with his physical condition has totally removed consideration to any other ability in this man's life. He is plagued by the perception of his limitations to sit, stand, walk, lift, bend and twist as he did prior to his injury. The inability to participate in sexual activity has diminished his impression of himself as a man. He considers himself a failure to his family because of his perceived role model influence. Recreational activities are severely compromised by his inability to withstand the required degree of physical activity. Not once, however, has the thought occurred to him that he will fight against the influence of his pain and physical limitations to take part in life. At no time has he said, "my pain, just for once, will not beat me." Alternative ways of performing activities are non existent in his thinking. Rather, the choice is made to resign himself to the hand dealt to him. When having a doctor's appointment, this he would attend. If physical therapy was recommended, he would follow the schedule. If the prescription was rest, he would comply. In the meantime, if no treatment was recommended, he would occupy his time the best way possible, which for this man consists of watching television.

For two years the mind of this man has been secondary to his physical symptomology. At 46 years of age, his life has been relegated to physician and physical therapy appointments and television. His ability to reason, no less, the way in which he could determine options for a more gratifying life, have not been considered. Now after participating in the various therapy programs, pain and sedation medication has become the preferred course to using whatever reasoning ability exists within him.

The profound feature in this man's chosen lifestyle is that to maintain this type of existence there must be a structure which has reinforcement. To gain mileage out of pain, sickness, and inactivity, support for the negative is necessary, otherwise, the pattern does not continue. For this man and others having chosen similar directions, financial remuneration, expected financial gain and personal vendettas have replaced using the reasoning ability of the mind.

Alternative choices can escape the traditional bounds of thought and provide a new awareness to future horizons. Because three generations of one's family subscribed to the belief that life has a predestined role for each member is no reason why individuals within the family cannot assert their own identity. Because the doors of knowledge have been shut to information which is uncomfortable is no reason to avoid seeking new understanding which supports use of one's potential.

## Life Enrichment as a Quest for Truth

During the course of a lifetime, countless decisions will be made by each individual shaping the destiny of that person. Additionally, each choice made will have universal relevance given the multiple lives touched by each action. Yet, very few will take the time to consider the reason for their existence or explore the nature of their essence.

By contrast, many will select the most obvious choice, where the human life is moved in accordance with the flow of the tide, translating to the latest apparel, the fad of the time, and the group with the most visible identity. Truth is measured in the consistency by which society standards are met, not in terms of individual contribution to the good of society or to the person, but by the recognition received from being in accordance with the standards of the day.

I was struck by an article suggesting the advent of gardening as the newest activity sweeping the country. While nothing is wrong with gardening, and in fact the activity is very worthwhile, I was intrigued by the sudden realization throughout the country of the sudden importance of this activity. I asked what makes this activity currently important? Does gardening spark some sense of creativity within the person through the recognition of "inch by inch, row by row, I see my garden grow"? Does gardening provide the needed topic of conversation so important to group identity? Or is the activity of gardening a means to create and nourish through one's personal effort? Perhaps gardening is the human attempt to regain one's roots which have been buried in the rubble of artificiality.

While the activity of gardening is used as an example, many other activities could likewise be used. The important recognition is why do we do what we do and are our actions anyway related to our perceived essence in life. This recognition sounds complex, particularly when confronted with daily struggles. Quite possibly, however, our personal struggle may be the direct result of never considering the basis for our choices.

I am amazed by the number of individuals I have had contact with in a professional capacity who have been literally manipulated in life to a point where complete personal control has been removed by them. Truth of life is determined by the quantity of neighbors' possessions as compared to their own, religious orientation of family and friends, and the comfort zone they allow themselves to experience without guilt. Questions of personal choice are met with answers of what would my friends think or say. Happiness, quality living, and purpose in life becomes weighed against the standards set by someone or something outside of the person. Personal control is only exercised when attempting to conform to group standards. Very effectively personal control is removed from determining the meaning of life and soon the quality of life suffers, unless a degree of callousness to personal feeling can be engineered.

In determining the meaning for one's life, at some point the reason for existing must be confronted. This is, if the desire exists to put yourself back in control of your life. If there is no problem with membership of a group in which your identity as an individual is preserved while simultaneously benefitting from the activities of a group, then by all means continue doing what makes you happy.

For those who wish to take direct responsibility for their happiness and develop the creative potential within themselves, exploring the issue of truth should likely become an integral part of their lives. This task is not necessarily easy, particularly if having difficulty realizing that truth is a highly individual phenomena for which there are few similarities. Comparisons of truth can become very frustrating when questions of whose standards of truth and what master plan is subscribed to are asked. The importance to any discussion of truth is the interpretation subscribed to by the individual. When interpretation is deferred to another person or ruling entity, caution must be exercised to preserve one's integrity.

The highly unique personal quality of truth can be illustrated through the following example. I received a call from a friend who indicated just having returned from an appointment with a neurologist relative to problems of facial paralysis and extreme pain in her jaw. Preliminary examination suggested the possibility of a brain tumor, to be confirmed by additional testing in the next several days. The symptoms had appeared suddenly but nonetheless were of intense concern to her. While acknowledging that stress had been a prominent part of her life the past several months, she could not ignore the physical symptomology and the impact on her life.

The prevalance of this physical condition, while devastating in terms of possible consequences, was viewed by this lady as a part of life to be addressed just as any other part. As with other events in her life, she had responsibility to give meaning to this event as it concerned her existence. The manner in which she dealt with this new situation was most remarkable. While showing genuine concern for her symptomology and the need for additional testing, she was excited about her plans to pursue training to become a travel agent, which included a change of careers for her. The development of a physical condition which had invaded her body was not to become the agent by which personal control would be removed.

As I listened to her discuss the new symptomology and perceived effect on her life, I was struck by the commitment she made to preserve the right to choose. Many others in similar situations would relegate themselves to the control of their physician, family and friends with exclusive focus on physical symptomology. The pattern of their lives is fairly predictable. Work would cease, happiness would end, and a variety of care packages would be delivered to ease the pain.

Meanwhile, personal responsibility would slowly degenerate to a point where control was relegated to the actions, choices, and self-serving interests of others.

The illustration of my friend clearly depicts the choice she is making to determine the meaning of the new experience and to use this event as an understanding of her overall purpose in life. The choice toward self determination is unmatched to any other choice which could have been made. The truth of this experience for her is that "I will take control for my thoughts, my body and my perception of the ultimate outcome of the events which happen in my life." In essence, truth for her is the perception and interpretation given to those events. Truth also, however, involves her direct attempts to continue moving on with life as reflected by pursuing another career, demonstrating the belief that truth demands recognizing one's evolutionary capabilities. In other words, by recognizing that her mood and spirit represent a distinct part of her evolutionary capabilities, she is continuing with an exploration of truth for her. Truth has consisted of movement, action, and participation; not lying in a hospital bed.

How similar to the experience of another lady who upon having x-rays was told of having a tumor in her bladder. Not to be denied with living life in the power of her control, she flatly stated that she would have more tests and, if surgery, chemotherapy or some other treatment was necessary, she would make the decision to the kind of treatment.

What she would not do is allow this experience to minimize her enjoyment of life. This attitude was demonstrated by her discussion of work and the contributions she was making, the plans for next weekend, and the values she wished to instill in her children. Truth for her consisted of invoking meaning into life which had lasting happiness and quality. Both of these traits were determined by the degree of her personal contribution and the pleasure derived from each experience.

Further tests revealed what was thought to be a tumor turned out to be a shadow. The experience, while ending positively, nevertheless, depicts the fragile nature of life which can change human reaction overnight. This type of experience also highlights the importance of capturing the meaning of each experience. No doubt, the scare of consequences with the potentiality of a tumor, heightens one's sensitivity to each moment, yet this possibility was not once viewed as beyond personal control.

The quality life which seeks to understand meaning for experiences is the life which recognizes that truth of experience is determined largely by the person. Obviously, there are environmental conditions, some of which are unexplainable, which alter the fulfillment of purpose; however, the actual occurrences of life are primarily the consequences of one's choices, perceptions, and actions. Standards of truth accordingly are the manifestations of one's experience as occurring to the individual. When the person is removed from the experience, truth soon becomes muddled in the perceptions of others.

One misperception in determining truth is that every conscious moment should be spent analyzing the essence of one's life. Certainly, no spontaneous action would emanate in that case. Yet there are many people who never seek to understand any element of truth. No thought is given to their happiness, contributions, or purpose. Life for them is mundane at best, with few episodes of genuine fulfillment of purpose. If purpose is discussed, the terms involve obligations. Responsibilities are to someone or a goal outside of the individual.

When the belief is maintained that ultimate truth lies within the understanding of the person, the integrity of personal choice will be preserved. Each day and every moment of our lives, new information and a greater depth of understanding is available. With this understanding, the truth of our lives unfolds. We see where we have been. We catch a glimpse of our future and our present becomes increasingly valuable for the fulfillment of ultimate purpose and direction for the future.

In determining what is truth, each person may wish to use happiness as a guide. Happiness serves a variety of purposes including purification, healing, and joy. The thought occurs that happiness may be the reason for and purpose of our existence. Consequently, ultimate truth may consist of pursuing a life, which at all costs, involves happiness.

## Enrichment from Uncommon Experience

A common tendency existing in life is to compare individuality with the norm of human experiences as judged by present day standards. Not uncommon is to measure identity by the style of our clothes, appraised value of our home and the car we drive. Taken to a fault is the apparent mediocrity seen within the peer group which emerges. As opposed to individual contribution is the shell of human existence composed of superficial elements from another time or the facade of current glamour.

A drive through most neighborhoods will attest to the values adhered to by those residents inhabiting the areas. Style of homes, automobiles, and recreational vehicles will represent a degree of similarity. Socioeconomic distinction will be readily observed by the outward manifestation of lifestyle. The homogeneous nature of the neighborhood, in fact is so apparent in terms of a cultural identity that any awareness of individual identity requires a close look at the subtleties of individuals living in a given area.

For those individuals choosing to avoid revolving around and riding the tidal wave of public hype, a different type of lifestyle ensues. The experience reflects long term investment of values where a significant part of the person has become part of the situation which has been encountered. The experience resembles the song which is played through the first time in its entirety by the composer, or the pilot who flies the plane he built for the first time. In a wonderful way, the experience provides an intricate level of personal involvement, unmatched in intensity with any other experience.

A friend was describing a recent trip taken to the Great Barrier Reef, where he and his wife had enjoyed the opportunity to snorkel, lie in the sun, eat good food, and enjoy the entertainment. The trip was relaxing and obviously therapeutic given the stress which he indicated as preceding this trip. As he and his wife discussed the events which they considered significant, I was intrigued by the corresponding lack of emotional excitement which these events implied. While they had been present for the events, their experience reflected more the experience of looking from the outside as opposed to being a part of the event. In contrast to a long lasting legacy from this vacation, the impression received was this trip provided confirmation of social expectations of someone in their peer group. The fact that a world under the sea had any reference to a deeper understanding of life and the human being's role in life was less significant to the fact that a trip to Australia had been taken. The impact of this trip was cursory at best. Less reference was made to the joy experienced from the trip as compared to the fact that the trip had been taken.

In retrospect, I thought how did that trip represent value to my friends. What can they say that they put in, gave to, and came back with, from that experience. In five, ten, or twenty years, will anything of substance be remembered, aside from the fact that a trip to the Great Barrier Reef was taken?

How different, I thought, from my recollection in the jungle along the Amazon, when observing the flight of an effervescent blue butterfly with a five inch wing spread moving through the trees. Not only was the appearance of this living entity striking but the simultaneous realization that I had a part in sharing and preserving this beauty. I thought how much move beautiful to see this free floating form of life in its natural habitat than to see a dismembered part hanging around one's neck in the form of jewelry or under glass in someone's home for purpose of ornamentation.

Some may suggest that life relegated to analysis of meaning prevents simple enjoyment from the experience. If the analysis prevents being a part of the experience, this occurrence is likely to be true. I have seen many people who worry so much about gaining meaning from the experience that the event which could have produced excitement, never happens. Similarly, I recall social occasions, where the strain of arranging a party preempted enjoyment at the party.

There is another type of person who is able to open the mind and senses of the body to allow for enjoyment and determination of meaning from the experience. On a trip off the coast of Papua, New Guinea, I saw 18 people from half way around the world realize the connection the island people of this territory have with their land, village and spirit. In no small manner did the experience of these islanders become a part of those 18 people making the trip. Each day for two weeks a sharing and understanding of the human experience occurred. Each person realized that every event and action was not an isolated event and that all of us shared this same world. In a major way, that experience leaves a lasting impression of hope, freshness and wonder.

The underlying belief for these individuals is recognizing that all life events are with purpose as is human behavior. The most insignificant is not haphazard. A friend once suggested that many times she performs activities without purpose. As an example she revealed the experience of browsing in different stores with no intention or purpose. For her the activity was spontaneous with no significance. I suggested she consider why she derived enjoyment from this activity.

Many of us never stop to consider the meaning of our experiences. Life is reduced to a set of responsibilities based on perceived expectations. Unfortunately, as opposed to deriving joy from such experiences, the reaction reflects boredom or the anticipation of an upcoming event. The time to stop and savor the encounter never occurs. Whether the experience is a trip to an exotic island or yard work on a weekend, the pleasure given to that encounter can only be given by the individual. At such times when the mind opens to meaning does understanding of personal existence began to emerge. Perhaps only for brief intervals is the awareness of contribution to life; however, these intervals are likely to be the most significant spaces of time during a lifetime.

## Personal Achievement Without Guilt

In the process of assisting others to identify and use their skills, I am amazed by how often I find a sense of guilt from being good at what they do. Many times when compliments are given, I have seen the remarks shuffled off as though the recipient was not worth it. Comments of "oh, it's nothing," or "it really wasn't that good" are not uncommon. Equally observed are reactions of embarrassment, as if something is wrong for being good.

How unfortunate the person who feels guilty for lack of productivity and guilty when making a contribution. Tragically, the malignant emotion sinks to a level of despair where only a conscious commitment to remove the growth, through the help of others, enables life to continue. A lady came to me complaining that her life was a failure. In the past two years she had been fired from two jobs and while she was currently working in another job, felt her termination was only a matter of time. She had begun taking classes at a local university without any real objective in mind. She considered her marital and family relationship good but recognized life for her involved more than being a homemaker.

The accomplishments of this 31 year old lady were discussed with her and not surprising was her tendency to down play these contributions to the extent of her failures. The impression that she had been a disruptive influence with her previous co-workers was much more significant in her life then the performance reviews depicting her quality in maintaining the security of the store for which she worked. No amount of attention to her contributions could offset the preoccupation with her failures. Every illustration of her contributions was met with a counter explanation of how she failed. She had very systematically made a case for her failures, which had become a way of life. Yet she could not understand why she perceived herself as a failure.

As the discussion continued, with increasing clarity, the influence of guilt in this lady's life revealed the direct cause of her unhappiness. She felt guilty over what she had previously done and guilty for presently being the best she could be. Her ability to move forward and achieve vocationally and academically was virtually stymied as a result of the weight of her guilt.

So often when observing the destructive influence of guilt is the wish to remove the core which sends out those "should and could haves". What a burden in which to live life when forced by the plaguing belief of being less then our capabilities or masking our potential for fear of ridicule. Many times the seed of guilt is the one comment reflecting our imperfection, which then germinates into a lifelong emotional state of despair. Parameters surround our commitment to using our potential. Limitations on our actions, desires, and beliefs are the result of our guilt as opposed to a quest for new understanding and improved value to our lives.

Enrichment from life is not possible with guilt. Guilt from utilization of potential can only serve as a malignant growth, barring any recognition of unlimited human potential. Guilt is the wall which stifles the mind from seeking a higher level of awareness and contribution. Guilt is the internal hate which results from repressing feeling. Guilt accounts for the death of joy. Guilt masquerades as sacred sanctity while promoting indifference in personal relationships.

Why feel guilty from personal accomplishment? What right is there to deny the mind, body, and spirit to limit the full expression thereof? The human being surely exists to use the mind and every sense to attain the fulfillment of joy. Without the pursuit of joy what purpose exists in life? Is life a probationary period where penance is the goal?

Why take time for guilt? Of what use is this emotion? Will we make ourselves or others feel better as a result of feeling guilty? Has guilt contributed to achievement or advanced the cause of human potential? The destructive nature of guilt is immeasurable. To continue feeding this emotion is to destroy the mind, heart and body in openness to the many opportunities awaiting us. The choice to abandon the guilt lies with us. Only by conscious intention and choice can this burden be lifted.

Any commitment to live life to the fullest of one's capabilities will necessitate living a guilt free existence. Life without guilt is not an easy task as there are many instances in which our bell can be rung and the right tones struck to elicit our sensitivity. Denying our children the opportunity to participate in an event or the personal pride which prevents an apology can easily precipitate the emotion of guilt.

There are means by which to avoid guilt, notably a good sense of self-esteem. Feeling good about oneself will counteract guilt. Insecurity is a prerequisite to guilt. The belief "I am not worth much in the first place" obviously will feed into the emotion of guilt.

Pride in ability and accomplishment is another way to ward off guilt. When one's focus is on reasons for not doing or participating in an event, the fuel for guilt exists. However, when individual contribution is looked on with pride, guilt has no room to exist.

Commitment to productivity will assist in reducing preoccupation with guilt. Realizing that productivity and guilt are counteracting forces, belief in maximizing one's potential through active participation in life will leave no time for guilt. Of caution in using free will are the revelators pronouncing that this selfishness can only lead to the demise of society. Unfortunately, they have not considered the contributions of these individuals adopting this stance.

There is life without guilt for those resolving to believe they were created with purpose. Guilt to them is an abstract phenomena which, if manifested at all, is like the sensation of a mosquito bite. There is no use giving undue attention to the sensation as in two to three days the bite will not be noticeable. More importantly is the realization that life is not lived for purposes of regretting but rather for enjoying. The sun does not shine in order for us to view the shadow of our failures but rather to illuminate our continuing achievements.

Believe in the rightness of one's actions.

# 7 The Reality of the Dream

One of the most beautiful experiences in life is to know that one's purpose is being completed to the maximum of their individual ability. To know that life is not being wasted and to receive fulfillment from one's work is truly a pleasure unmatched. Unfortunately, only a small percentage of the population will ever recognize this achievement or their potential to make this a reality. Life for them will remain a reactive phenomena where the majority of time is spent responding to the innovations of others and maintaining a life according to contemporary standards.

How much more can life be to know that the short time spent on this earth could be packed with gratifying experiences, the results of which are due to our direct investment. What a marvelous realization at anytime in one's life to know a contribution is being made which improves the well-being of all society and which will be of value when they are gone. In the twilight of life to realize a monumental contribution has been made and more is to come is a most consoling awareness.

The formula to understand, fulfill and realize one's purpose in life varies according to each person. Unique abilities and differences account for a variety of combinations which bring a plan into being. For some there is the ability for scientific involvement, while others are more suited to interpersonal activities. The variations in purpose expand to the number of human beings on this planet, for each person brings a unique gift to the world in which they live.

Despite the individuality of each person, the realization of purpose, potential and dreams are made possible to a greater degree by understanding the format by which potential can evolve. History is filled with classic examples of men, women, and children who believed. Fortunately, they chose to ignore the adage of "the idea is before its time." Presently, the lives of individuals who also believe in themselves and their purpose are illustrated by their actions. In a significant and magnificent way they have revealed the potential of the human mind and the will of the spirit. In the face of defeat, they have defied failure and internally said, "I will move forward." When others have given a host of reasons why an idea, plan, or activity will not work, an excuse for abandonment has never been part of their ideology.

The success of these individuals has not happened by chance. While some would believe they were predestined to stardom, closer analysis would suggest differently. First, there was an element of self-confidence where an openness to personal potential existed. Second, there was an awareness to new opportunities. Opportunities were sought out. Third, they had a plan to complete their purpose. Fourth, a way to sustain the energy to maintain this plan was in place. Fifth, they learned to enjoy their accomplishments.

Unfortunately, in a world filled with examples of the cruel and inhumane, the human spirit is denied the opportunity to create. The appeal of violence, exploitation and mechanization toward the common deny the spirit a sense of autonomy. Disproportionate focus on evil manifested by indifference replaces efforts taken to improve the quality of life. The bombing of a village is given more attention than the efforts of several individuals strategizing a plan for peace.

With disgust, but not ignorance, are reports of violence heard. Preoccupation with disease at the expense of health is considered a blight on the life seeking to be lived. In contrast to emphasis on what is wrong is the need to consider what is right. The belief that nothing good comes from focusing on the wrong must be central to the person.

A recent reminder of the quality which life offers and which in turn we infuse to life occurred during a recent father's day outing. The day with my son was filled with time in the mountains where we had the opportunity to examine wild flowers in the meadow, observe the contrast of a green landscape of grass and trees, interspersed with purple, yellow, orange, white and red flowers, with the backdrop of snow covered mountain peaks encased in clear dark blue sky. As a bonus to the day was the opportunity to sit in a natural hot springs while taking in the splendor.

The opportunity to experience this phenomena is sensational when alone, but reaches unparalleled proportions with a twelve year old son. In a wonderful way the spontaneous joy felt at that time sustains itself at other times when life becomes a bit too constraining. The experience, however, reveals the opportunity to realize our unlimited potential alone and with those we love. To communicate without an agenda and to avoid interruptions speaks to the deeper sense within us that emerges with the message "move forward and act on the belief which will sustain you and the world."

Despite the fact that the following morning I would be in my office and later in the day in some distant city, my mind, body and spirit had the opportunity for rejuvenation in a way which could conceivably never be recaptured. The time together with my son in an environment which was in harmony with our experience, was symbolic of a chemical interaction with each form of life. The thought which recurred was, you have to believe in this goodness for without this belief within you and in life itself what good is life? If life is lived to be destroyed, why exert any effort to continue living?

Equal to believing in the goodness in life is the contribution within us all, to end our acts with a positive exclamation mark. The happy and satisfied people I have met demonstrated these two basic principles. Giving has had no sense of obligation or an expectation of return on investment. They have known the benefits of any action will far exceed the energy expended. They have known a destiny which will be denied at no cost, and for some the cost was great as family and friends simply could not understand.

Often the pursuit of a dream is responded to by others as a self-centered scheme which denies others some central part of their being. This assumption could hardly be further from the truth of personal dream accomplishment, as I personally know of no one who has not involved others, either in a supportive or facilitative manner, in achieving their purpose. Rare indeed is to find the human being isolated to a point where the full utilization of potential is possible without assistance from others. In my experience, the practice of assisting individuals to develop and use their skills has repeatedly revealed the social need of the human being to accomplish their purpose and incorporate others into a dream.

The need to have others involved in a dream while retaining a sense of individual integrity is well illustrated by the comment of a friend who indicated in her own life, the longing to have someone with whom to share her zest for life. After twenty years as a musician and instructor, she now desired to use her skills in a different capacity of greater magnitude. Realizing her life had reached a level of comfort and the fact she could settle into a life of complacency, she could not deny the sense of the spirit which suggested a life of further accomplishments. While realizing the art she had taught to so many students and the joy brought to others through her concerts, there was yet another part of her life necessary to her destiny.

What a beautiful example of passionately living life free of artificial constraints. The relaxed but yet vigor in her voice, the brightness of her eyes, and the freedom with which she allowed her mind to exercise all revealed she could not be denied from achieving her purpose. A person who had risen to the top of her profession and realizing the value of her past success, now dedicated to attainment of one more goal.

Interesting, however, to this lady's experience was the lack of clarity she felt in what her future purpose was. The argument could be made that her sensation was some change of life which occurs in every person at a given stage of life. To her this explanation was unacceptable. All she knew was that the sensation existed with the reason for the sensation being less important at this time than the fact the sensation existed. The marvel of her attitude was the commitment to an openness of each experience and sensation no matter what the basis. How many other individuals with the potential to have this type of experience can say the same?

Realizing that feelings and excitement occur for a reason, she did not remain exclusively in an emotional state, but rather began using her mind to develop an expanded understanding of her potential to where she could evolve to a higher level of productivity. She considered her past experience, the friends she could use as resources and professional expertise from colleagues in her field to understand the purpose and means to completing her purpose. She began identifying a plan with specific people, a timetable for completion of certain goals, and a refinement of the service she wished to offer. She also recognized attainment of a dream and completion of purpose happens in its own time which enabled her to continue focusing on options to use her capabilities without losing hope.

So what has she decided as her current mission? In answer to this question, she described her sense of using music to universally help others create. She expressed how music breaks the dogma of religious, cultural and socioeconomic bias, and how music can be used as one tool to uncover hidden potential within a person. She has seen the need in people striving for this ideal and realizes a place will emerge which will provide an opportunity to use her talents.

As I sat and listened to her description of reaching others through music, I became enthralled by the prospect of people throwing away the mental chains of confinement and experiencing the benefit of latent abilities heretofore untapped. I also thought of my own experience of learning to play the piano after the age of 35, and realizing what a tremendous treasure to be able to read music and play a song. I thought if this is possible for me, how much can be possible for others with similar interests. I also thought what a wonderful source of relaxation the acquisition of this skill has had in my life. While I am not a concert pianist, nevertheless, the pleasure to me of making a choice to take piano lessons will never be replaced.

To this woman and others making the commitment to continue growing, there is no false pretense, no superficiality, and no fear of failure. In no small way is she incorporating her technical skill in music with the larger responsibility of helping people understand their potential. Music is essentially the medium. She fully realizes the trauma which has beleaguered many people, who otherwise would be capable of exercising their potential to greater accomplishment. By listening to an arrangement of Brahms or Mozart, the blues, or a rendition of folk songs recorded in the '60's, perhaps the seed of germination for the person exposed to music will take hold.

Questions of dreams, purposes, will of self and God, are difficult. Many a person will believe the combination of events suggests a specific purpose only to have those plans fall through. Not uncommon is the statement heard "but I did everything right." I recall working with a man who received a large financial settlement for a work related injury and at the time was convinced he would be "settled for life". He intended to purchase a new car, pay off his house and other smaller loans, invest part of his money conservatively, and live off the interest. Possibly, if there was money to spare, he would start a small business, although he was not sure in what. Less than two years after the settlement he was broke.

One of the downfalls to this man was when he turned his life completely over to others. Everyone who knew him had a plan for what to do with his money. There were business opportunities by the dozens requiring a limited investment of $20,000 to 30,000. The appeal of one new car soon was joined by a new pickup and then a boat for recreation. Some actual investment, although relatively small in proportion to the settlement, was placed in a money market fund, however, slowly that was taken out to meet living expenses.

I received a call from this man's wife after most of the money was gone in reference to job possibilities for her husband. Apparently, the preceding two and one-half years had been spent buying with minimal consideration to his purpose in life. At the age of 35 his ship had come in. Unfortunately, the ship only remained in port approximately two years before departing again.

After several discussions with this man's wife and subsequently with him, a plan to return to a life of productivity was arranged. The plan involved an initial level of self sacrifice but more importantly a commitment to look beyond the material pleasures with which he had surrounded himself. While explaining these "treasures" were not evil in themselves, the fact they replaced his true value in life required a change of thinking. The last contact with this gentleman revealed him to have regained control of his life and back on the road of using his skills to the most appropriate extent possible. He had found a job and created a budget which he could live by, two of the most essential ingredients of life for him.

The two individuals just described could reflect the same experiences for many people, some choosing to see the reason for their evolution and others waiting to be acted on by fate. The issue with either person is not to prove to society the justification of their actions, as is the need to live in accordance with exercising one's potential. Without being true to oneself, how can one be true to any other element of life? If authenticity within the person is non-existent, how credible is anything emerging from that individual?

A plan to determine purpose, act on a dream, and fulfill our destiny has a special uniqueness to the individual. With the wide biological, intellectual, cultural, social and attitudinal differences existing among us, a master plan for enacting one's potential is questionable.

Perhaps, however, there are several suggestions which can lead each of us toward that right combination which will open the gate to our dream. First, we must closely consider information which is presented to our senses. Whether we feel, hear, touch, see or smell, even in a vague sense, this information is vital as it leads to the second step of formulating a plan. The data which is presented to us by way of ideas, people we meet, news broadcasts, or songs, all has specific meaning to our present and future purpose in life.

Third, once a plan is prepared, the need to execute this plan is necessary. One of the most difficult aspects I have observed in life is the ability of a person to be proactive; in other words, to make things happen or show initiative. Rarely, if ever, have I seen a passive recipient with a reactive attitude fulfill a destiny consistent with utilizing one's highest potential.

Fourth, while our destiny belongs to us, the fact any action taken will affect the rest of the world must be understood. For example, if our purpose is to facilitate peace, surely the comments made in daily conversations will have a far reaching impact to many areas of the earth. There is an interdependence of all life manifested by a multitude of forms within nature which also speaks to the soul of each person when pursuing the highest purpose intended.

Fifth, a time for reassessment of objectives is necessary. During the course of a lifetime the host of varied experiences, new insights, and an improved understanding of potential and options available will occur. Consequently, an openness toward the possibility of modifying a plan cannot be discounted. Of concern, however, is to never lose sight of the destiny which is known to be true.

Sixth, while time is necessary to seek out answers from the mind and soul, there is also a need to seek out those individuals sharing a similar commitment to our dreams. While their dreams involve a different direction, the fact they have an excitement is substance enough to warrant their involvement. At a time when a plan is beginning to grow, there is not time for a defeatist person telling you the plan will not work or is before its time. This is not, however, to deny counsel who can clearly provide objective information on the feasibility of the plan. The benefit of having those key people share your dream is the energy they contribute in rejuvenating and keeping the ideas which you know to be true taped to the inside of your forehead.

Finally, once a specific action is taken, be satisfied this is the best action which could have been initiated at this time. Too often an action is taken, only to have the author of that action plagued by worry and despair. This can only cause undue stress and prevent the continuation of creative energy for developing extended facets of the dream. To be happy and satisfied with personal accomplishments is one of the greatest gifts we can give to ourselves. Let us not deny ourselves the opportunity to do this for us.

# More Quality Books from R & E Publishers

**WHO IS THERE TO SHARE THE DREAM?** Finding Purpose & Potential After Tragedy by Dr. John M. Janzen. Life doesn't have to be over when tragedy strikes. Dr. John M. Janzen should know. In 1969, he was diagnosed with malignant bone cancer and told he had only six months to live. After numerous operations and radiation therapy, his leg and hip were amputated. Today, he snow skis, scuba dives, travels the world, and lectures around the country. He is the president of a company that helps the disabled to develop new skills and re-enter the work force. This book is written for anyone who has ever suffered a setback or disappointment. It is inspirational and practical.

| | | |
|---|---|---|
| $9.95 | LC 91-50687 | ISBN 0-88247-899-0 |
| Trade Paper | 6 x 9 | Order #899-0 |

**ON LINDA: Love, Loss & Renewal** by Edward T. Milligan. Captain Edward T. Milligan's wife did not have to die. Although she needed a liver transplant, she was only 31 years old and her overall condition was good. After a year and a half wait for a suitable donor organ, the end came suddenly and unexpectedly. She might have been saved if there had been enough blood from black donors available.

"On Linda: Love, Loss & Renewal" is a non-fiction novel that chronicles her brave struggle and her family's journey through grief and tragic loss to strength and recovery.

This novel is especially important for minorities. Milligan shows how a shortage of blood and organ donations from blacks, Hispanics and other minorities has led to a health crisis that causes thousands of needless deaths each year.

| | | |
|---|---|---|
| $11.95 | LC 91-50694 | ISBN 0-88247-898-2 |
| Trade paper | 6 x 9 | Order #898-2 |

**WHAT WORKS:** 5 Steps to Personal Power by William A. Courtney. Life is simple—if you know *What Works* and what doesn't.

This power packed action guide is a handbook for creating your dreams. Based on time tested universal principles, this book will guide you through the five steps of personal power. Once you master these simple principles, you will be able to create anything you want, from better health, to financial success, to deeper, more loving relationships.

| | | |
|---|---|---|
| $7.95 | LC 91-50983 | ISBN 0-88247-910-5 |
| Trade Paper | 6 x 9 | Order #910-5 |

**THE SEARCH FOR MANHOOD:** A Guide for Today's Men & Women by Scott Leighton. *What does it mean to be a man?* Men's roles are changing in our society. As women seek greater equality and power, men now look for greater depth and meaning. This collection of humorous and hard hitting essays will help men, and the women in their lives, to reach a greater understanding of what it really means to be a man. It examines the most vital issues in the lives of every man—work, family, sexuality, emotions and the legacy of boyhood. This pivotal work will help men to give themselves permission to feel and express the entire range of emotions, from love and anger, to joy and despair. It will release them from the bondage of socially imposed roles that have forced them to be only half alive.

| | | |
|---|---|---|
| $6.95 | LC 91-50986 | ISBN 0-88247-916-4 |
| Trade Paper | 6x9 | Order #916-4 |